ETHICAL ARGUMENT

ETHICAL ARGUMENT

CRITICAL THINKING IN ETHICS

SECOND EDITION

HUGH MERCER CURTLER

New York   Oxford
OXFORD UNIVERSITY PRESS
2004

Oxford University Press

Oxford   New York
Auckland   Bangkok   Buenos Aires   Cape Town   Chennai
Dar es Salaam   Delhi   Hong Kong   Istanbul   Karachi   Kolkata
Kuala Lumpur   Madrid   Melbourne   Mexico City   Mumbai   Nairobi
São Paulo   Shanghai   Taipei   Tokyo   Toronto

Copyright © 2004 by Oxford University Press, Inc.

Published by Oxford University Press, Inc.
198 Madison Avenue, New York, New York 10016
www.oup.com

Oxford is a registered trademark of Oxford University Press

Library of Congress Cataloging-in-Publication Data
Curtler, Hugh Mercer.
    Ethical argument : critical thinking in ethics / by Hugh Mercer Curtler.–2nd ed.
    p. cm.
    Includes bibliographical references and index.
    ISBN 0-19-517316-3 (pbk. : alk. paper)
    1. Ethics. 2. Critical thinking. 3. Decision making–Moral and ethical aspects. I. Title.
BJ1012.C87 2004
170–dc22   2003066216

Printing number: 9 8 7 6 5 4 3 2 1

Printed in the United States of America
on acid-free paper

For Linda

CONTENTS

FOREWORD

Ethical Argument: Critical Thinking in Ethics is a special book. It is unique, timely, nondogmatic, and refreshing in its tone. It is a perfect supplementary, perhaps even primary, text to use in an introductory ethics course or a course in critical reasoning.

The book is unique in that it combines the subjects of ethics and logic/critical reasoning. Occasionally I have a student who takes my Philosophy and Social Ethics course simultaneously with my Introductory Logic course, which emphasizes critical reasoning. When this happens, I find myself giving "asides" to this student in both classes, relating the material from the other class to what we are discussing. I point out that, in an article in our ethics textbook, so-and-so is giving a particular type of argument which, as the student has learned from the critical reasoning course, should be evaluated in a particular way, or the author is committing a certain fallacy that we studied in the critical reasoning course. The student taking both courses simultaneously clearly has an advantage over the other students taking one class alone. In the ethics course, the student has the tools to summarize and evaluate the arguments we study, and in the critical reasoning course, the student has more interesting and philosophically important arguments to which to apply what he or she has learned than the usual canned exercises in critical reasoning texts. Hugh Curtler has realized that students studying ethics need critical reasoning tools to evaluate the arguments that are given. I would, further, argue that given the importance of ethics in our lives—Nietzsche maintained that human beings are essentially "valuing animals"—those who study critical reasoning should be able to apply what they learn to ethical arguments, so time should be spent discussing how to evaluate ethical arguments in critical reasoning courses. I know of no other book that combines ethics and critical reasoning as this book does.

Curtler himself uses critical reasoning in this book to present a timely argument leading to a conclusion that is not only important for the study of ethics, but essential if we are to discuss ethics at all. He rejects the position of ethical relativism, the view that there are no objective ethical truths, that ethical beliefs express no more than personal or, more likely, cultural biases. Curtler argues that those who would force us into accepting ethical relativism because the only alternative is to accept the view that ethical claims can be made with certainty, which doesn't seem to be true, are committing the fallacy of creating a false dichotomy. There is another alternative: Good reasons can be given for accepting certain ethical views, so these views can be considered to be true until better arguments can be given to reject those views. Curtler's entire book can be seen as presenting his case for accepting this other alternative, by showing us that we can make a distinction between good and bad arguments in support of ethical judgments. Good arguments, in Curtler's view, avoid fallacious reasoning and rest on facts and three central ethical principles: respect for persons, fairness to others, and the adoption of rules that increase the sum of human happiness.

Curtler's rejection of ethical relativism is timely because we are currently suffering from a moral crisis in America, largely as a result of the general acceptance of ethical relativism, which is a by-product of the "politically correct" doctrine of "multiculturalism." Multiculturalists maintain that it is important to celebrate different cultures so that everyone feels valued and appreciated. This view—which has not allowed us to be critical of any culture's values—has conditioned most Americans to accept the cultural form of ethical relativism. Ethical relativism seems to be the "tolerant" position to take, in opposition to the "rigid" view of ethical objectivism. People think that defending ethical objectivism will give dogmatic people license to impose their own code of values on everyone else. But, as Curtler points out, in accepting ethical objectivism, one is not saying that anyone now has all the correct answers on ethical matters. One is simply asserting that there are correct answers that we should be trying to discover. Few philosophers accept ethical relativism because, to quote Curtler, "relativism tends to end all discussion of what may be right or wrong before it even starts (what's the point? who's to say?)." The study of ethics is only possible if we assume the truth of ethical objectivism, rather than ethical relativism. It is to Curtler's credit that he clearly defends this thesis. It is a message that students need to hear, and seldom do, even in philosophy courses. In general, philosophy instructors have been trained to play devil's advocate and criticize each view that is discussed, so we tend to turn our students into moral skeptics.

There will be those who are critical of Curtler's rejection of ethical relativism, and this is fine with him as long as they can find an error in his reasoning. Curtler does not assert his views in a dogmatic fashion. With every point he makes, and this includes his rejection of ethical relativism, Curtler challenges readers to think for themselves and not necessarily agree with everything he has to say. This is one of the best features of the book. Curtler himself presents possible bases for criticizing the points he makes in his excellent "Food for Further Thought" sections throughout the book.

The refreshing tone of this book will be welcome to students. This is a book aimed not at fellow professional philosophers—needing to be translated by the instructor so that students can understand it—but at the students themselves. Curtler manages to do first-rate original philosophy, in arguing for his main thesis, in an accessible, friendly, thought-provoking manner, always asking the reader, "What do *you* think?"

Susan Leigh Anderson
University of Connecticut

PREFACE

TO THE INSTRUCTOR

This book is an exercise in what might be called the epistemology of ethics. It focuses on the question of how we can know that our claims in ethics are true or false. Bertrand Russell distinguished between two separate functions of words, use and mention, and my approach *uses* argument to make a point while, at the same time, it *mentions* the techniques that are necessary to put together and take apart strong arguments, generally.

The reader may object to the fact that I have an obvious ax to grind in that the book is clearly an attempt to undermine ethical relativism. But the approach is not dogmatic; the reader is constantly urged to question the main thrust of the argument, consider alternatives, and put together arguments of his or her own that are independent of mine. This is accomplished by adopting the Socratic *maieutic*, or what Karl Popper called the method of "conjecture and refutation." The main argument is presented in the form of conjecture, which the student (or instructor) is encouraged to refute if possible. This way, it is hoped, the student will acquire critical thinking skills, while at the same time standard critical thinking skills are being taught in the text itself. Again, this is an attempt to combine the two functions of use and mention.

In this way the book is unique in its approach to ethics, and it should be adaptable by instructors who are either sympathetic with this approach or totally opposed to it—in that it can be used as a foil by those who disagree with it, or it can be used by those in sympathy with my concern with what I see as widespread ethical relativism among undergraduate students. One of the main advantages of this text, other than those already mentioned, is the fact that it is brief enough to allow supplementary material to be used in a typical semester system. This is by design. Instructors who want a more theoretical approach can supplement the text with primary sources;

instructors who want a more practical approach can supplement the text with more case studies in areas of their main concern; or, finally, instructors can take an entirely different tack and supplement the text with novels and short stories, or even items from the daily newspaper, to give the course a more lively focus that will capture the imaginations of their students who sometimes fail to see the relevance of theory to what they like to think of as "real life."

ACKNOWLEDGMENTS

I would like to thank my colleague Stewart Day, who taught the first edition of the book several times and then made a number of helpful suggestions for improving the second edition. Also, two former students, Kevin Stroup and Jill Anderson, read an early draft of the manuscript and made a number of helpful suggestions. I thank them for their assistance as well. And I would also like to thank Professors Kriste Taylor, Mark Smillie, and Wallace Beasley for carefully and critically reading the manuscript in its entirety and suggesting numerous changes that resulted in a much improved text. I am also grateful to Professor Susan Anderson for her willingness to write a Foreword to the second edition.

I want to give a special thanks to the computer wizard at Southwest Minnesota State University, Shawn Hedman, who was able to somehow transform ten-year-old floppies containing the first draft into workable type for the second edition.

And finally, I am particularly grateful to my wife, Linda, who put up with (an even more than usually) preoccupied husband for months on end and then read the manuscript carefully and made certain that the material was presented in the clearest way possible.

Several of the forty-two case studies in Chapter Six are from the "Report of the Committee for Education in Business Ethics" sponsored by a grant from the National Endowment for the Humanities in 1980 and do not have a copyright. I thank Norman Bowie, nonetheless, for giving me permission to use those cases. While most of the remaining cases are original, several have been borrowed from Michael Bayles' book *Professional Ethics*, © 1981 by Wadsworth, Inc. They are reprinted by permission of the publisher and are noted in the text. The "Doonesbury" cartoons, © Gary Trudeau, 1984, 1985, 1986, and 1987, are used with permission of Universal Press Syndicate, as are the "Calvin and Hobbes' cartoons, © 1989 Universal Press Syndicate.

INTRODUCTION

TO THE STUDENT

I should begin by noting that the term "argument" as it is used in this book refers to a thoughtful procedure for stating conclusions and finding the best possible support for those conclusions. It doesn't mean what we usually mean when we argue with our friends about which movie we should see tonight or who is the best basketball player ever to play the game. It doesn't even require that we raise our voices!

By presenting a series of arguments that are designed to persuade you that ethics is a suitable arena for rational deliberation, this book asks you to seriously question relativism in ethics. The arguments seek to show that ethics is not just an arena for conflicting personal opinions or feelings and differing cultural perspectives, as you may think. It is hoped that by presenting the book in the form of an extended argument, you will be encouraged to think along with me and to sharpen your critical thinking skills at the same time you are learning some effective critical thinking techniques.

I will adopt the Socratic method that stresses the need for criticism as a *positive* means to more reliable conclusions. This method was called *maieutic* by the Greeks. It involves careful scrutiny of truth claims and the rejection of those claims that cannot withstand criticism. The remaining claims can be considered "true" unless or until further criticism dislodges them. This is not to say that truth can be *defined* in terms of non-falsehood; a claim is not true just because it cannot be shown to be false. That would mean that if the claim "Caesar had freckles" cannot be shown to be false it must be true. But the same thing could be said about the claim "Caesar did not have freckles," and this would be absurd. Something cannot be both true and false at the same time and in the same respect! What I am saying is that a claim can be *considered* true if we cannot show it to be false. It is true *as far as we know at present*. In ethics this is often the best we can do, but it is considerably better than simply saying that truth and falsehood have no place in ethical conflict and it's all a matter of opinion.

One way of looking at the critical examination of ethical claims and counterclaims is to imagine yourself at a trial as a jury member who knows that a crime has been committed but who doesn't know who did it. You must listen to the evidence and weigh it carefully before reaching a conclusion "beyond a reasonable doubt" as to the identity of the guilty party. The main problem with this analogy is that ethical claims like "Sally *shouldn't have* murdered the milkman for leaving whole milk instead of skim" are different from factual claims like "Sally murdered the milkman for leaving whole milk instead of skim." Some say the differences are so important that any attempt to liken ethical investigation to determinations of matters of fact—as in the case of a jury trial in which there clearly is a guilty party—is bogus: Ethics is about personal feelings, not about facts. These critics insist that ethical claims are not "truth claims," or claims that purport to be true; they are simply statements about how we *feel* about things that happen—I get upset when I think about Sally's having murdered the milkman and that's why I say it was wrong.

This criticism would reduce ethics to a purely subjective, or personal, level, a view that is carefully scrutinized in this book. So also is the related view that would reduce ethical claims to statements about shared feelings and attitudes in a given culture or subculture. Clearly, there are feelings involved in ethics, and certainly it is the case that our ethical pronouncements frequently reflect those feelings. It may even be the case that occasionally our ethical judgments are *nothing more* than an expression of our feelings or the feelings of those among whom we live. But does it follow from any of these statements that ethical judgments can be reduced to those feelings *in all cases?* That is to say, we can admit that subjective factors such as personal feelings enter into ethical judgments without allowing that there is *nothing else* involved. There may be excellent argument support for the claim just made that Sally shouldn't have murdered the milkman—aside from the fact that thinking about it upsets us. Before we decide that the ethical claim is merely a "matter of opinion," or simply an expression of feeling, we need to see whether or not there is any support for it and, if there is, to examine that support.

> The question of whether ethical claims are "subjective" or "objective" is decided on the grounds of the support (or lack of support) for those claims, rather than on the claims themselves.

This is the view that will be defended in this book. Rational support for our ethical claims is called "justification." The objectivity of ethical judgments, then, is a function of justification: To the extent that we can justify ethical judgments, they are objective; to the extent that we cannot justify these judgments, they are subjective, or relative.

One of our chief concerns in ethical argument, then, is to see if we can find evidence and argument support for the claims we make in ethics. If that support is strong, and if it is not *culture bound*, that is, accepted by people in one specific culture and not generally accepted in other cultures, then anyone at any time should follow the argument and accept the claim that comprises the argument's conclusion. If the claim commands our consent because of the compelling nature of the support for that claim, then we can say with some confidence that the claim is not simply a matter of personal opinion or cultural perspective: It is "objective." As the British philosopher Karl Popper has said, "objective means *justifiable*, independently of anybody's whim: a justification is 'objective' if in principle it can be tested and understood by anybody."[1] Whether or not I *want* to accept a reasonable conclusion, I *must*—if I am honest, open-minded, and capable of following the argument. What we seek in ethics are precisely those elements and features of an ethical argument that we are compelled to accept whether we want to or not, "independently of anybody's whim."

Much of what goes on in this book will be centered around the question of justification in ethics. Since justification is a matter of evidence and argument support, we will want to know what makes arguments strong or weak, how to forge strong ethical arguments, and how to undermine weak ethical arguments. What are some of the most common fallacies we make in putting arguments together? We will want to know what constitute "good ethical reasons" in support of ethical arguments and how to weigh reasons *pro* and *con* to reach plausible ethical decisions.

The success of my attempt to undermine ethical relativism will depend on whether or not I can make my case on behalf of sound reasoning in ethics. We shall see whether or not strong arguments provide escape from the morass of conflicting opinions and feelings which, for many people, seem to be the whole of ethics. I do not contend that ethical claims can be made with certainty, or that any one of us is in the privileged position of having **The Truth** in ethics. But I question the position of the relativist that would leave us with no reasonable way to resolve ethical conflict and no sensible way to make ethical decisions. I seek a middle ground, acknowledging the uncertainty that surrounds ethics without giving in to the temptation to throw up my hands and conclude that the uncertainty is ineradicable.

In saying this, I must reveal an assumption that is being made here. It is assumed that "reasonable" approaches to ethical conflict are preferable to "unreasonable" ones. In speaking about "reasonableness" I follow the American philosopher Brand Blanchard, who said,

> By reasonableness I do not mean intelligence, though that may be a great help. Attila, Torquemada, and Stalin were highly intelligent men, but they were not reasonable men. Nor is a reasonable man necessarily a learned man, for learning may be present without even ordinary common sense. No; the reasonableness of which I am speaking is a settled disposition to guide one's belief and conduct by the evidence. It is a bent of the will to order one's thoughts by the relevant facts, to order one's practice in the light of the values involved, to make reflective judgment the compass of one's belief and action.[2]

Whether or not you find this plea for reasonableness and its attendant rejection of relativism convincing, I would hope that you will at least suspend judgment until you have carefully considered the arguments presented in these pages. The ultimate goal of this book is to encourage readers to reach their own conclusions about ethical reasoning by means of a critical examination of the book's central argument.

Is it possible to liken ethical reasoning to a jury trial in which someone is truly guilty or innocent? That is to say, is there anything like a *fact* at the center of ethical conflict to which we must consent because of the nature of the evidence for that fact? Or is ethics reducible to a jumble of personal opinions, none of which is any "better" than the others? These are the central questions that confront us as we begin our examination of ethical argument.

PLAN OF THE WORK

After a brief dialogue between Rick and Nina, two imaginary students who worry about whether or not people in one culture are ever in a position to make value judgments about activities that take place in another culture, the book begins with a careful discussion of ethical relativism. The view is defined and criticized in Section One of Chapter One, and the counterthesis—namely, that ethical judgments when carefully grounded in evidence and argument are not relative to persons or cultures—is defended. In the third section of Chapter One, I try to determine the limits to which we can claim that ethical judgments are nonrelative, or objective. It is suggested that in ethics, as in the case of history and even the exact sciences, subjective or personal elements enter into our judgments, but we need not allow that ethical judgments (any more than historical or scientific judgments) can be *reduced* to those personal elements.

In Chapter Two I examine several ethical principles that will provide a framework for the discussion in the remainder of the book, as they have in ethics generally for many years. I propose that respect for persons be regarded as fundamental in ethics and that fairness be added, together with the admonition to adopt a rule that will maximize human happiness (consistent with respect and fairness) in order to adopt ethical options and resolve ethical conflicts. This discussion gives rise to an examination of "The Ethical Perspective" from which we can see more clearly how such conflicts are to be resolved and such choices made. The ethical perspective requires that we ignore short-run self-interest and practical considerations (for a time); we must seek a perspective that is disinterested and cognizant of the long term and allows us to imagine ourselves in the place of the victims of iniquity.

After a brief "interlude" to look in on our imaginary students, Rick and Nina, I begin to forge the tools of ethical argument in Chapter Three. I examine the structure of arguments and the factors that contribute to strength or weakness in those arguments. The second section of Chapter Three presents a number of the most common informal fallacies that we should be aware of in trying to structure sound ethical arguments and reject weak ones. It is followed by exercises designed to help the student hone his or her critical skills.

The heart of the text lies in Chapter Four, in which I examine in considerable detail the process of justification in ethics. Justification is contrasted with rationalization and explanation and provides the grounds for claiming objectivity in ethics. Those ethical claims are objective that we can support with evidence and argument in a way that can withstand criticism and appeal to a neutral audience . . . such as a jury in a crime trial. This is the focus of the fourth chapter and of the text as a whole.

In Chapter Five four case studies are presented in some detail as students are given an idea how to approach ethical conflicts critically and how to put together sound arguments of their own.

The final chapter provides more than forty cases in a variety of subject areas, from sports to medicine, for discussion and analysis.

NOTES

1. Karl Popper, *The Logic of Scientific Discovery,* New York: Harper and Row, 1968, p. 44.
2. Brand Blanshard, *Four Reasonable Men,* Middletown, Conn.: Wesleyan University Press, 1984, p. 247.

ETHICAL ARGUMENT

Setting the Stage

Opening Dialogue

In order to get our discussion under way, consider the following imaginary dialogue between two students who have just left a philosophy class not unlike the one you are taking.

RICK: It's interesting reading a book like Chinua Achebe's *Things Fall Apart* in an ethics class. It raises some very knotty questions, and it makes you see someone else's point of view. That is something we all need to do from time to time. We get bogged down in one way of looking at things and think it's the *only* way.

NINA: Yes. I agree. But Achebe's book is based on fact, more or less, and there are some things about what goes on in Umuofia, the village Achebe describes in his book, that really disturb me.

RICK: Oh? Like what?

NINA: Well, for example, his protagonist is a wife-beater and a child-abuser. Also, the people in his village leave twin infants in the "evil forest" to die because they think the babies are possessed by some sort of spirits. That's just not right! In some ways, even though the coming of the English causes things to "fall apart," in other ways it was an improvement. For one thing, they saved the infants' lives.

RICK: Whaaat!!?? How can you say such a thing? Here you are standing outside your comfortable American classroom making a judgment about another culture on the other side of the world. You may not like what they do, but that's *your* problem. What right do you have to say what the people in a small village in Africa should and should not do?

NINA: It's not really a question of "rights" is it? I mean, don't we have a responsibility to speak up if someone is doing some-

1

thing that is obviously wrong—in our own culture or anywhere else for that matter?

RICK: I don't think so. Not at all. It's like the rules of a game. Many of the white people in Africa are of English decent and they like to play soccer, which they call "football." The rules of soccer aren't the same as the rules of what we call football. But who's to say which are the "correct" rules? They probably do all sorts of things differently from the way we do them. Who's to say we're right and they're wrong, or vice versa? You shouldn't be so judgmental.

NINA: Well . . .

RICK: Let me give you a different sort of example. We just read about this in our history class. When the U.S. invaded Panama and overthrew Manuel Noriega the military leaders of the U.S. Army insisted that the Panamanians keep a strong military presence to provide security for the Panama Canal. The people of Panama themselves wanted no Army at all, or at most a very weak military presence, because they had been under strong military rule for twenty years and they wanted no more of it. Now I ask you: What right do we have to tell them what's good for them?

NINA: Wait a minute! Don't go so fast! You are confusing three things: infanticide, games, and the advice of our military people to Panama. I would agree with much of what you say about games, and insofar as no one gets hurt many of the customs and practices of other countries are like games. Who cares about what their marriage practices are, for example? The case of the Army in Panama is more like a game than is infanticide, because it's more a question of tactics than anything else and presumably no one gets hurt. If someone does get hurt, then things change radically. And when babies are left in the forest to die, we might not only object, but we might very well recommend intervention in order to prevent this sort of thing—and to help preserve the rights of the innocents in that country. I would agree that involvement in another country's business is always wrong, unless there are compelling ethical reasons. But I'm not advocating intervention here: I'm simply saying they are wrong. I'm making an ethical judgment, and you're saying I have no "right" to do that. I say that when people are being hurt or killed that is grounds for ethical condemnation. It's possible that intervention is also called for, but that's another matter entirely.

RICK: But what you call "wrong" is not recognized by the people of Umuofia, as far as we know. You want to impose your ethical views on them.

NINA: Only if my ethical views are *correct.*

RICK: But how can you know that? There is no such thing as a "correct" ethical view! There are only my ethical views, yours, and the people of Achebe's village who live on the other side of the earth. There are clearly differences among them, but none is any more "correct" than the others. It's all relative.

NINA: Relative to what? To culture?

RICK: Yes, for the most part. We are all products of what anthropologists call "enculturation" and we take in attitudes and beliefs with our mother's milk. We aren't even aware of what those attitudes and beliefs are half the time! We certainly don't question them: We assume them and in the end we fall back on them because they seem self-evident. All your fancy talk about "right" and "wrong" is simply a thinly disguised verbal camouflage for what is nothing more or less than a cultural prejudice.

NINA: You are saying that the concept of human rights, for example, is nothing more than a cultural prejudice?

RICK: Yes, if you must.

NINA: But a prejudice is something that precedes judgment and excludes reasons. On the other hand, the claim that humans have rights is one that I can support with reasons that *anyone* should accept, not just those in my culture. Clearly there is a difference between these claims and others that cannot be supported by reasons and which cannot withstand criticism—claims that clearly *are* nothing more than bias in this or any other culture. Your view collapses all claims to the same level as bias or prejudice. That's ridiculous! You're getting carried away here!

RICK: I'm not sure what you mean. Give me an example.

NINA: Let's suppose I'm a teacher and you are a student.

RICK: OK. I'll go along with that. But I think you've got it backward!

NINA: Clever! Anyway, as a teacher I belong to what is, technically, a subculture of a culture we'll call "Academia." We'll call that subculture "T."

RICK: Agreed.

NINA: And in my culture there is another subculture "S" made up of students just like you.

RICK: OK.

NINA: Members of my subculture agree that henceforth we will all evaluate the work of our students in the following fashion: Those sitting closest to the front of the room will receive "As" and those sitting closest to the back of the room will receive "Fs" and those sitting in between will receive corresponding grades.

RICK: You mean, those sitting in the second row will get Bs and the third row Cs and so forth?

NINA: Yes.

RICK: No way! That's ridiculous! It's totally unfair.

NINA: Why do you say that? Members of my subculture have agreed on this procedure, and if the students don't like it they can leave and go someplace else where things are done "fairly."

RICK: But your group's determinations are arbitrary and capricious. Anyone can see that!

NINA: That's *your* opinion. But don't forget you're not in my culture. What right do you have to say we're not being fair?

RICK: *Anyone* can see it's not fair! Grades in your system would no longer represent anything meaningful: There would be no relation whatever between the grade and performance. Knowledge would count for nothing. Students wouldn't be motivated to study anything; they would simply fight for seats in the front row. That's an absurd example!

NINA: Is it? Or is it just like infanticide? Aren't the students in subculture "S" just like the people in Achebe's novel? At least, aren't they like them in important respects? Aren't you getting all upset here because the example involves people like *you* and you can identify with them? As long as the issue doesn't effect you it is easy to sit back and make pronouncements about how it's none of our business. But think about it: The reasons you gave (that my grading system is arbitrary and capricious) are reasons you think *anyone* in any culture should accept! And you're right! Those are *good* reasons in that they are binding on people in my subculture as well as those in your subculture. They certainly aren't disguised prejudices as you said earlier: They have nothing to do with culture.

RICK: But they do, in a way. My subculture recognizes these reasons, whereas yours does not.

NINA: Yes, but my subculture *should* recognize these reasons, don't you think? I mean, after all, the faculty's decisions affect you and the other students as well. Indeed, my subculture should recognize *any* truth claim that is supported by reasons, in ethics or anywhere else for that matter. If people in my subculture insist that our grading system is fair after they have heard your arguments against it they're a bit like the members of the Flat Earth Society, who insist that the earth is flat even though the evidence doesn't support that claim. Your reasons for rejecting our grading system are like the reasons given in the sciences against the flat earth hypothesis: Their appeal cuts across cultures. And you are right; our grading system would be grossly unfair. The appeal is in some sense universal. Anyone who follows the argument and weighs the evidence *should* accept the conclusion.

RICK: Perhaps so. But they won't, and you know it.

NINA: You're right. I do know it. But that's beside the point. It's for the psychologists to tell us why it is that people don't accept as true those things for which there are strong reasons. Why do people continue to believe that the earth is flat? I don't know. Do you? That's not our problem.

RICK: Yes, but I still think the strength of those reasons is a cultural phenomenon. Strong reasons in one culture will seem weak in another culture. To go back to our original example, what possible meaning does the phrase "human rights" have to a group of people for whom blacks are not even human?

NINA: Ah yes, but that's a question that can easily be settled by the biologist. That's a fairly easy matter, and like many of the reasons that support ethical claims, it's a matter of fact. The easiest way to handle the question is to examine the supposed reasons that support the claim that blacks are *not* human. We see whether these "reasons" can stand up to criticism: That's how we proceed—propose and dispose. Examine the evidence, sift through it, and accept only those reasons and that evidence that can withstand criticism. This is not a cultural matter; it is a matter for any reasonable person. Good reasons are culture-blind. And clearly we cannot find any good reasons for denying black people their rights, even though this was done by whites for centuries. We have to say the whites were blinded by prejudice and were simply wrong in this case.

RICK: Perhaps so, and perhaps not. Surely cultural bias enters in. There's no way to avoid it at some point in the argument. Aren't you likely to consider *anyone* who disagrees with you as "unreasonable"? Isn't your position likely to lead to intolerance, an unwillingness to consider any position that conflicts with your own "reasonable" position?

NINA: That's a possibility, of course. But that's the point of the method of proposal and disposal: It's supposed to be used to examine my own convictions as well as those of others who disagree with me. It may well be that *I* am being the unreasonable one. It doesn't have to be the other person. Personal and cultural bias can crop up anywhere, and it is important that we keep an open mind and eliminate it anywhere we find it. We may never be entirely rid of it, but criticism will help us get rid of much of it, and more each time we reconsider our arguments, we would hope.

RICK: Then what you're saying is that the "truth" of ethical claims is a matter of more or less, not either/or? It is a matter of strong reasons, or good reasons, which are always more or less infected with cultural bias. Is that it?

NINA: I think so. But I'm not sure I know what you mean by truth being a matter of "more or less" and not "either/or."

RICK: Well, you know. In math, for example, the statement 2 + 2 = 4 is either true or it's false. There's no middle ground. In psychology, if we say that "a person who lives in a densely populated area is more liable to become violent than if the same person lived in a rural area" that statement is more or less true, again, depending on the weight of the evidence. Technically, such claims are either probable or improbable rather than true or false. Their probability is a function of the evidence: The more evidence there is to support the claim, the more probable it is. What you're saying is that ethical claims are more like the claims in psychology than they are the claims in mathematics. Right?

NINA: Yes. That's it.

As the title of this chapter suggests, this dialogue sets the stage for the remainder of the book. A great many students who come to ethics for the first time tend to take Rick's position, pretty much as I have presented it here—although they might not give in quite as easily to Nina's arguments! For that reason, I will try to persuade you that Nina espouses the stronger position. You may or may not agree, but one of the rules of the game is that you must try to see both sides of the issue as you proceed and keep an open mind. Whether or not you come to agree with Nina in the end, you will have done some serious thinking about ethical issues and ethical points of view—and that's what is most important!

CHAPTER ONE

Is It All a Matter of Opinion?

Relativism versus Objectivism

1.1 CLAIMS IN ETHICS: A CRITIQUE OF RELATIVISM

Historians of science tell us that relativism began to permeate Western thinking in the late nineteenth century. At that time non-euclidian geometry had begun to challenge the classical view "that all knowledge was unitary. If one found a kind of certainty in geometry, then one could hope for the same kind of certainty in physics, in biology, in ethics, or in religion."[1] In conjunction with non-euclidian geometry, Darwinism, scientific naturalism, and the new sociology and anthropology made it possible by 1900 for William Graham Sumner to state categorically that "there is no natural law; there are no natural rights, and there is nothing a priori. The only natural right is the right to survival."[2] The term "natural rights" was the term used for many years as an equivalent for "human rights," and "natural law" was equivalent to "moral law." In rejecting these two notions, the relativist was rejecting any sort of objectivity in ethics. And if ethics cannot be regarded as, in some sense, "objective," then, in the words of Martin Luther King, Jr., there is no moral high ground.

As a consequence of this assault, relativism has become so prevalent in our day that it is not restricted to ethics or morality. It has worked its way into our everyday thought and appears in a variety of guises. As Nancy L. Gifford tells us:

> Naive relativism is certainly alive and well in the idioms of our ordinary language. "True for you, true for me" is echoed in "to each his own," "everyone is entitled to his own opinion," "when in Rome do as the Romans do," "different strokes for different folks," and "whatever feels good," to cite but a few examples. We use these id-

8

ioms casually and comfortably. There seems to be little need to ask ourselves what we are really saying. In fact, we might not even consider ourselves relativists when we use these expressions. . . . They become a familiar part of our environment. We can expect that just the repetition of such relativistic expressions can produce in the speakers of the language a predisposition to uncritically accept or prefer relativistic positions on the grounds of familiarity (sometimes called "common sense").[3]

Given this background, it behooves us to take a close and critical look at ethical relativism, since there is obviously a great deal at stake. On the face of it, some things do appear to be right and others wrong: There does seem to be moral high ground. And we would all like to think that, on occasion, we stand on it.

Relativism in Ethics

For the aforementioned reasons, the prevailing view in our culture is now that judgments in ethics, and value judgments generally, are "relative." Many people share Rick's view in the preceding dialogue. For such people, ethical disputes are merely conflicts among various and assorted desires, wishes, interests, attitudes, and likes or dislikes, all of which are relative to the individuals involved in the disputes or, perhaps, to their respective cultures. Thus, according to such people, if I judge that the Nazis were perverse in wanting to annihilate the Jews, or that the young Palestinian was demented when he walked into a crowded restaurant in Israel and blew up himself and a dozen other men, women, and children, that is merely my "opinion"—which is a collective term we use to include all or most of the words in the long list just given. According to the popular view, these "opinions" are not subject to rational argument beyond cultural boundaries, and, according to this view, ethics currently wallows in a quagmire in which reason has no place. As the Marxist writer Terry Eagleton put it, ethical relativism leaves "itself with no more reason why we should resist facism [for example] than the feebly pragmatic plea that facism is not the way we do things in Sussex or Sacramento."[4]

I shall subject this view to careful scrutiny with an eye to rejecting it and insisting instead that there is a place for reason in ethics, an important place, and that ethical reasoning can help us find our way out of this quagmire of conflicting opinions, that it can indeed help us to solve many of the ethical problems that confront us in today's complex world, to find and take the moral high ground. This is the claim I make in this book, but it is not one the reader should take at face value: It is one the reader will be encouraged to examine carefully and critically at every juncture.

What Are Ethical Claims About?

The central issue in the relativism/nonrelativism issue is over the question of whether value judgments are about subjects and/or cultures, on the one hand, or about events and objects in the world independent of those subjects and cultures, on the other hand. That is, if I say, "Brutus was wrong to have killed Caesar," am I saying something about myself (subjectivism), about my culture (cultural relativism), or about the event itself (nonrelativism, or objectivism)?

In the first case, the judgment either expresses my personal antipathy toward the event ("That kind of thing gives me the creeps") or else it states a claim about my attitude toward the event ("It is true that I disapprove of that sort of thing"). In the second case, the judgment makes a claim about the dominant attitude in my culture toward such events ("Generally speaking, such things are not acceptable in my culture: It is against the law"). In the third case, the judgment claims to be about the event itself—regardless of my likes and dislikes or those of the people in my culture ("It is wrong for Brutus to have killed Caesar").

> The determination of whether we are making the judgment from a relative or nonrelative stance depends on the kinds of reasons given for the claim in every case.

For the subjectivist/relativist, the reasons support the claim that one does, in fact, disapprove of such events—or there are no reasons because there is no judgment, merely an expression of one's feelings about the event in question. For the cultural relativist, the reasons support the claim that persons, generally, in that person's culture do, as a matter of fact, have (culturally bound) reasons for disapproving of such things as killing. That is, the reasons are convincing only to those, or most of those, within that particular culture. For the nonrelativist/objectivist, compelling reasons support the claim that the action was wrong and anybody at any time from any culture whatever should agree with those reasons and conclude the same thing about that event, regardless of their personal or cultural predispositions.

The Truth of Ethical Claims

For the relativist/subjectivist, value judgments can be both true and false—true for you (or your culture) but false for me (or my culture). "You say it was wrong for Brutus to have killed Caesar, I say it was not." On the face of it, that's an attractive position, open-minded and tolerant of different points of view. But, unfortunately, there are limits to tolerance, and there are things that most people, if not all, would agree are simply wrong (we would all try to stop a man beating a very young child if we caught him!). And it makes sense to try to figure out what these things are that most people agree about and whether we have good grounds for suspecting that they are, indeed, wrong. Unfortunately, relativism tends to end all discussion of what may be right or wrong before it even starts (what's the point? who's to say?), and this is the main problem with the view, from the philosopher's perspective. For the objectivist, on the other hand, value judgments cannot be both true and false: They are either true or they are false for the reasons given, or other reasons as yet to be determined.

Objectivism, then, opens up the discussion, since the claims that are made (such as "Brutus should not have killed Caesar") are arguably true or at least reasonable; consequently, there is something to discuss, something to agree or disagree about; whereas, for the relativist, there is not.

The tricky thing about the differences between relativism and objectivism is that they cannot be determined by simply looking at or listening to the way the claims are expressed: The claims all look the same! As mentioned earlier, the difference is found in *the kinds of reasons* given in each case. Thus, the question "Why?" becomes pivotal in ethical reasoning. Let us look more closely.

A. Relativism/Subjectivism

"Brutus was wrong to have killed Caesar."
"Why?"
"Because I just feel that way. That sort of thing makes me sick. I can't stand violence. Yuk!! etc. etc."

The claim is about the speaker, or writer, and is therefore subjective or relative to the subject.

B. Cultural Relativism

"Brutus was wrong to have killed Caesar."

"Why?"

"Because people in my culture don't do that sort of thing. It is illegal and morally repugnant to people like me. I have always been taught that sort of thing is wrong."

The claim is about the speaker's culture (and himself or herself as a part of that culture) and is therefore culturally relative.

C. Nonrelativism/Objectivism

"Brutus was wrong to have killed Caesar."

"Why?"

"Because it violates ethical principles concerning respect for life, principles regarded as basic to any culture and most major religions."

(OR)

"Because Brutus miscalculated the effects on Rome and the action produced the opposite effect from the one he intended and resulted in pain and suffering for a great many Romans that might have otherwise been avoided. Thus, even if one tries to justify the action itself in terms of consequences, those consequences show that the action was wrong."

This is a nonrelative claim that is supported by reasons and argument that are accessible to anybody at any time—regardless of one's personal or cultural bias. The truth of the claim is a function of the strength of the argument support. Instead of debating the claim itself, then, we must take a look at the reasons given to support that claim. Note how examining reasons makes sense in the case of objectivism, whereas it really doesn't in the other two cases. What point is there in asking what reasons one has for thinking Brutus was wrong if those "reasons" are accessible only to me or others in my culture?

In all three cases, claims are being made. But in each case the claim is different and that difference must be determined by examining the reasons and evidence provided. We shall denote the difference by referring to "relative claims" and "nonrelative claims." In doing this, we shall consider subjectivism and cultural relativism as two types of relativism and as fundamentally alike, even though the latter view is more plausible than the former and therefore needs to be taken more seriously. In any event, both views contrast sharply with nonrelativism, or objectivism, which is the view I am defending here.

Justification in Ethics Is a Function of Support

In ethical reasoning, what we are looking for, then, are what the eighteenth-century German philosopher Immanuel Kant referred to as "objective and sufficient" grounds for ethical judgments, grounds that make those judgments acceptable to anybody who considers them carefully and critically. In a word, we are seeking "justification" for our ethical judgments. If this justification is to be nonrelative, it must be objective in the sense that the grounds or support for the claims that purport to be justification must be able to withstand rational criticism from *anybody*.

It is certainly the case that it is *difficult* to justify ethical judgments, or value judgments generally—since we cannot see things like "greatness" and "wrongness" and don't know what, exactly, corresponds to the judgments in question. Nevertheless, when I say "Shakespeare was a great writer," it is quite possible that there is *something* in the plays of Shakespeare that allows us to attach the term "great" to those plays, and to their author, in a sensible way, once we have agreed what we mean by the key term "great." Our attention can be drawn to those features of his plays as we try to determine what we find there that is missing in the works of, say, Jackie Collins. This is what literary criticism is all about. Usually we try to give compelling reasons based on a close and careful reading of the text, and to eliminate bias and prejudice as far as we can. We also look for factual evidence, and it is these reasons and this evidence that comprise the rational foundation for justification in the arena of values. The fact that we might disagree about the strength or weakness of this rational foundation does not imply that our value judgments about Shakespeare, or murder, are hopelessly relative or subjective. In fact, we might go so far as to say that value judgments that engender the most lively debate are precisely those that are most worthy of being considered meaningful and significant claims.

Let us be clear about what my main contention is: Ethics involves nonrelative claims, that is, claims that are either reasonable or unreasonable. To the extent to which an ethical judgment is capable of rational justification and support that is not culture bound it is an objective claim, although I admit that the *process* of justifying ethical claims and removing relative elements, such as personal bias, admits degrees of success or failure. It is difficult (although not impossible) to become aware of our own biases and emotional attachments. Thus I admit that the claims we make in ethics are *more or less* relative, depending upon whether or not we can identify and remove subjective and cultural elements such as these very biases and emotional attachments. I concede this much to the relativist. Cultural bias and prejudice, together with often fierce emotional commitment, enter into value judgments more often, perhaps, than in any other type of judgment. But these subjective elements can be identified, and to the extent to which we become aware, for example, that our judgments are based on cultural bias and passionate commitment, we can free ourselves from those elements and see if there is any rational (cross-cultural) basis for the claim. If I come to realize that I am homophobic, for example, then my judgments about homosexuals are likely to be flawed. But if I can recognize and eliminate this bias, then my judgment is more likely to be correct. This is, to a large extent, what ethical reasoning involves; this is what "justification" involves in the ethical sphere—the elimination of bias and prejudice along with other subjective or relative elements from the support we give to our ethical claims to see if there is any objective basis for those claims, anything that anybody else *should* agree to and accept for good ethical reasons.

If we can agree, then, that there is a difference between nonrelative and relative claims and that we do (or we can) make nonrelative claims in ethics, and to the extent to which these claims can be justified they are objective, we must now confront the more difficult issue of how we determine, in a specific case, whether we are dealing with a relative claim or a nonrelative claim and, if the latter, how strong that claim is—how prevalent the subjective and relative elements are in the evidence we provide for that claim. Note here that the term "strong" refers to the degree of objectivity an ethical claim is able to achieve by way of rational argument and the support of independently testable, compelling evidence. The freer the support for a claim is of personal and cultural bias and the more compelling the argument and evidence are to rational, disinterested persons, the stronger that claim is; the less evidence and support for a claim and the more prevalent the subjective and/or cultural elements, the weaker the claim.

The procedure of verification or justification is fairly straightforward. We try to isolate and identify objective elements in our judgments just as we try to identify and eliminate subjective or relative elements. The latter are those elements that are peculiar to the subject making the judgment or are relative to that subject's culture and are not, therefore, binding across cultures on all rational persons. When we make objective claims, then, we can say they are true, or reasonable, to the extent that

---

1. We can verify them or falsify them ourselves at another time.

2. Someone *else* (regardless of that person's cultural biases) can verify or falsify those claims.

3. The claims can withstand rational criticism.

These three steps involve the gradual elimination of subjective and cultural elements and the identification of those elements in our judgments that are objective, cross-cultural, and impersonal. The method is not perfect, but it can be quite successful. It involves proposal and disposal, criticism and defense, modification and adaptation. Above all else, it requires an open mind and intellectual honesty.

Food for Further Thought

The thesis offered here is a difficult one to swallow—especially if one is in the habit of dismissing ethical or aesthetic judgments as mere "opinions." The notion that we can make judgments of the sort "Shakespeare was a great writer," or "Brutus was wrong to have killed Caesar," and insist that these are claims that can be justified rankles many people. It seems to many to imply that we are saying we have superior knowledge, that we know things that others don't know. You may want to ask: Are you saying that Shakespeare was a *better* writer than Jackie Collins? But that is absurd! I love to read Collins and find Shakespeare totally boring. Furthermore, one of Collins' novels outsold all of Shakespeare's plays put together! Who's to say that Shakespeare was a better writer? Indeed, how can we say he was "great" when we don't know what that means?

These are good questions, and such questions will recur in later chapters where I shall attempt to deal with them directly. For the moment I can only point out that there is no claim to superior knowledge implied in the position defended thus far: No one is saying that he or she *knows* (for sure) what makes Shakespeare "great." The thesis here is that Shakespeare either is or is not great—he cannot be both—and Brutus either was wrong or was not wrong to have killed Caesar. Whichever view is correct can be rationally defended by anyone who wants to take the time to determine what is distinctive about Shakespeare or about the situation surrounding Caesar's assassination.

The road ahead in this book is not easy. Ethical reasoning takes concentration and effort, as we have already seen. But if we are convinced at the outset that it is impossible—if we start from a relativistic stance—there's no point in further discussion! So at the very least we should allow, at the outset, that it is *possible* to engage in ethical reasoning, to discover rational foundations for our ethical judgments. If after making the attempt we decide it cannot be done then we shall be in a position to say so.

One important point should be noted in passing. It is much more *interesting* and more fruitful in the long run to insist that value judgments are objective claims and not merely personal beliefs than to give in to the popular tendency to reduce them all to personal beliefs or opinions. The objectivist thesis (which I am defending in this book) opens many doors to investigation that would otherwise be kept closed. If we insist that value judgments are merely personal beliefs then the only one who needs to consider them is the one who asserts those beliefs, his or her close circle of friends and family, and, perhaps, his or her psychiatrist. If the judgment isn't about our shared world it holds no philosophical interest for the rest of us. It seems a mistake, however, to relegate all value judgments to this sphere. As N. L. Gifford so nicely puts it, "It is an unfortunate consequence of the relativistic positions that they ultimately encourage us to turn away from the larger world about which we are so curious."[5] To put the matter differently, relativism is a pernicious doctrine, since it ends discussion before it can begin by insisting that there is no *point* to that discussion, no possible outcome. If, on the other hand, we can treat value judgments as reasonable beliefs or objective claims about our common world then we can discuss them, agree or disagree about them, and settle disputes about them—at least in principle—in a rational manner. Reasons and evidence support these claims and either do or do not make the claims objective. Thus it is the evidence and the reasons given to which our attention must be directed, the "objective and sufficient grounds" for the judgment. That is, we can engage in ethical reasoning if we are willing to ask the question "Why?" and can pursue the response with an open mind.

1.2 THE CASE FOR OBJECTIVISM IN ETHICAL ARGUMENT

Asserting that ethical relativism is unacceptable and that ethical judgments can be reasonable claims and not simply personal beliefs is one thing; making the case for this assertion is another.

To begin with, we need a better grasp of what it means to say that ethical judgments are, or can be, "objective," and a better understanding of how, as specifically *ethical* judgments, they resemble and differ from other types of judgments. Because of the obvious differences between ethical judgments and, for example, ordinary judgments of perception we tend to dismiss ethical judgments as merely "relative" and, for the most part, to regard perceptual judgments as nonrelative or objective, and as such either true or false. Although the differences are certainly quite real, there are important similarities as well, and we need to attend to these to be fair in our assessment of ethical judgments.

In the last section, I broadened the scope of our discussion a bit and spoke about Shakespeare's "greatness." Let's now restrict our discussion to the framework of ethics. My point will be the same, although I need to focus the discussion more sharply. If I say "George is a good man," that is very different from saying "George is over six feet tall." I can see and measure height, but I cannot see or measure "goodness." Does it follow from this, however, that I have no reasonable grounds for making the *claim* that George is a good man? That is, can I provide no evidence for claims other than that provided by sensory experience—what can be seen and measured? Or is there more to verification and justification than mere sensation?

Possible Parallels with Other Disciplines

Let us take three very different judgments, one from astronomy, one from history, and one from ethics, and let us see what constitutes verification, or justification, in each case. In doing so we should note the similarities as well as the differences; if I am to make the case that ethical claims are nonrelative claims, I must know how to verify claims I know to be nonrelative and see whether anything like that occurs in the case of ethical claims.

My first example is from astronomy, and it states something none of us is likely to question:

> (C1) "The earth encircles the sun annually in an elliptical orbit."

The second example is a historical claim:

> (C2) "Greece and Sumeria were closely linked during the late Bronze Age."

The third example is from ethics:

> (C3) "Radar detectors should be outlawed."

Whether or not the third claim is true is irrelevant for my present purpose. In saying that it is a "claim" I am simply saying that it *claims* to be true; that is, there is a procedure for testing it and for accepting or rejecting it as true or false based on the evidence that supports it. That is, it can or cannot be justified. To see how we might justify the third claim, we need to see how this takes place in the more straightforward examples from science and history.

Scientific Claims

In the example from science (C1) we have a judgment that is not, strictly speaking, based on perception. The evidence that supports the claim is mostly from mathematics and physics. Much of the sensory evidence cannot be relied upon because it "cuts both ways": It can be used to support either the geocentric or the heliocentric hypotheses, as they are called. The sun's apparent movement can be accounted for either by the motion of the earth or the motion of the sun. The mathematical evidence, however, is almost entirely on the side of the heliocentric hypothesis, suggested by the Polish astronomer Copernicus. Therefore his hypothesis can today lay claim to the title of "the more reasonable view."

Copernicus first proposed the theory that the earth encircled the sun in 1530 A.D. His proposal met with a mixture of support and violent opposition. The support resulted from the fact that he had already established his reputation as a mathematician of considerable ability. The opposition resulted from the fact that his theory was in direct conflict with the traditional view of the Roman Catholic Church, which on the authority of Aristotle put man in his "rightful" place at the center of the cosmos. The opposition ran deep. Fifty-seven years after Copernicus' death Giordano Bruno was burned at the stake for defending the heliocentric hypothesis. Even Martin Luther chastised Copernicus, calling him a "fool" for holding views contrary to the Bible. Copernicus' response courageously admonished "those who are completely ignorant of mathematics and yet dare to judge such questions, and who will blame and reject my work, relying on some badly interpreted passage of Holy Scripture."[6]

Not until new discoveries in mechanics, more accurate mathematical calculations, and the more precise astronomical observations of such thinkers as Tycho Brahe, Galileo, and Johannes Kepler in the early seventeenth century did the heliocentric hypothesis gradually begin to displace the older geocentric hypothesis that went back to Ptolemy and seemed on the face of it to accord with common sense and reason. Galileo, for example, was able to show that bodies continue to fall in straight lines even if the earth itself is in motion, and he also discovered four moons circling Jupiter in a way that seemed to provide a model of the solar system as a whole. In addition, the Copernican view was simpler, requiring only thirty-four circles to account for the motion of the earth, the moon, and the planets, as opposed to the seventy-nine circles required by the Ptolemaic hypothesis. The point was placed beyond reasonable doubt by Newton, whose laws of motion made it possible to explain the attraction of bodies toward the center of the earth and the attraction of large bodies to one another across great distances. This explained why we don't fly off into space as the earth circles the sun and why the earth itself doesn't fly off into infinite space in a straight line—matters of great concern to the opponents of the heliocentric view!

In the end, the Copernican view was supported by new observations, increased accuracy, greater predictive power, simplicity, and inclusiveness in its ability to accommodate other claims—all of which, taken together, seem to form a coherent whole. The logical considerations of coherence and consistency, which had been acknowledged as far back as Aristotle, lent force to the new view of planetary motion.

Perhaps just as important as these considerations that led to the final acceptance of the Copernican hypothesis of planetary motion was the fact that the observations and calculations could be repeated by *anybody* at *any time*. This is the criterion of "testability," which is central to the process of verification and the establishment of claims as objective and not merely as personal beliefs.

The mass of evidence since Copernicus, and especially since Newton, has elevated the Copernican system—modified by Kepler's notion that the planets travel in elliptical orbits—to the level of truth and Kepler's original theories to laws. Such cannot be said for historical claims, as contained in the second case (C2). But the process of verification for such judgments, while certainly not as rigorous and exact, is not altogether different—as a moment's reflection will attest.

Historical Claims

Take the historical claim that "Greece and Sumeria were closely linked during the late Bronze Age." As Karl Popper has argued, historians proceed to verify this sort of claim not by tracing its sources or its origins, "but [they] test it much more directly by a critical examination of what has been asserted—of the asserted facts themselves."[7] Consider the historian at work in the following passage by a contemporary American historian. In reading this, pay particular attention to the way the historian collects evidence to support his or her claim.

Raphael Sealey's book *A History of the Greek City-States 700–338 B.C.* shows innumerable examples of the procedure Karl Popper has described. For example, Sealey attempts to argue that Hesiod's *Theogony* shows close ties with the Sumerian *Epic of Kumarbi* and that therefore Greece and Sumeria were closely linked intellectually during the late Bronze Age. In supporting his claim, Sealey presents the following argument:

The time of composition of the *Theogony* is not clear; a date in the eighth or seventh century can be defended. But the date when it reached its present form may not be important, since it was composed orally in a traditional technique. It presents ideas of the kind which could reach Greece at the time when the alphabet was borrowed and orientalizing styles of pottery began. It is indeed conceivable that the story of the successive generations of gods was borrowed as early as the late bronze age, to which the Hittite text of *The Epic of Kumarbi* belongs, but this is less likely; the complexity of the story would not be easy to preserve in Greece of the dark ages, when contact with eastern lands was slight. The proper conclusion is that in the early archaic period, as in the late bronze age, Greece belonged to a single cultural and intellectual circle of the Near East.[8]

Try to tear your mind away from the fascinating subject matter and consider, for the moment, the *method* Sealey uses in this passage. It appears that Sealey is doing precisely what Popper says he should be doing: He is criticizing alternative points of view, rejecting those that seem unreasonable, and accepting only that conclusion that remains after criticism. Note the language of what Popper calls "critical rationalism." In this brief passage, the author uses the following key phrases: "can be defended"; "which could reach Greece"; "It is indeed conceivable"; "this is less likely"; and "The proper conclusion is."

The historical method is thoroughly rational: Historians look for inconsistency and incoherence—does the claim fit in with the body of accepted historical facts? If it does not, it is likely to be false. (It is possible that the body of known facts is in error, but more likely that the new claim is so if it doesn't fit in.) Historians also look for evidence of bias on the part of the individuals who provide historical testimony. In rejecting Julius Caesar's accounts of the customs and social organization of the Germans, for example, the English historian/archaeologist Malcolm Todd points out that

> it must be remembered that Caesar was not primarily a dispassionate ethnographer. He was an aspirant for the highest political offices and to the historian such men are dangerous.[9]

In addition, historians look for unreasonableness and unreliability of testimony and/or the sources of information at their disposal. Later in his book, for example, Sealey is critical of some claims made by the Greek historian Thucydides about the reasons for the beginnings of the Peloponnesian war. He notes, "One should be skeptical of unrealized intentions [attributed to the Spartans by the historian], especially when they are said to have been secret; such allegations could not be checked and could be invented later."[10] Indeed!

Clearly the critical methods of the astronomer and the historian differ, but it would be a mistake to focus only on the absence of mathematical proof in history and the social sciences generally and to therefore overstate those differences. The methods of the scientist and the social scientist are thoroughly rational; both seek objectivity and reject bias, unreasonableness, and falsehood.

Possible Analogy with Ethics

In the sciences and social sciences, the methods of verification involve reliable methods of observation and calculation combined with a critical awareness of the context in which a claim is made and in terms of which the claim can be seen to be plausible or implausible, coherent or incoherent, consistent or inconsistent. These are methods of rational investigation that require reasonableness and reliability as determinable by *anyone* capable of undertaking the investigation. They are not subjective and they are not culturally relative, either.

Analogous methods are used in ethical justification, and ethical claims must be weighed and examined with the same critical scrutiny, the same insistence upon reasonableness and reliability. And the process must be repeatable by anyone at any time. Ethical claims are "objective" to the extent that they avoid bias and the rational support they rest upon is impersonal and interpersonal and at least approximates the same standards of reasonableness and reliability we would require of any claims anywhere—whether we are determining historical accuracy or the shape of the orbits of planets.

Even though there are some problems involved in drawing parallels between science and ethics, the stubborn fact remains, after all is said and done, that some ethical claims are stronger than others; some are absurd while others approach self-evidence. More importantly, perhaps, many ethical claims can be supported by reasonable arguments and evidence that command the respect and assent of people of good will anywhere and at any time.

Ethical Claims Examined

Let us take the case of the ethical judgment in our third example involving the radar detectors and see how we might provide a reasonable foundation for this claim. In what way can we consider the judgment "Radar detectors should be outlawed" to be a nonrelative, or objective, claim and not a merely personal belief or a claim relative to our culture?

To begin with, as I noted in the first section of this chapter, if we ask the question "Why" in the face of this judgment three things can happen. In the first case the speaker simply says, "I don't know. It just seems to me to be the right thing to do." In this case we are faced with a subjective claim, a claim that simply reflects the feelings of the speaker, because it lacks rational support. In the second case, the speaker may proceed to note the customs or rules that prevail in his or her culture and that lend support to the claim that such things are not approved of in that culture. In the third case, however, the speaker may list arguments and evidence to support the judgment that cut across cultural boundaries in their appeal to all rational persons. In this case we have a nonrelative claim if, and only if, the evidence and support for the claim is not culture-bound in some way. That is, the claim purports to be true not only for our culture, but for any culture whatever. It is our job to see whether or not the support is adequate, that is, whether or not the claim can withstand critical scrutiny. We shall employ the Socratic *maieutic* and (most importantly) focus our attention on the support for the claim rather than the claim itself.

With this in mind, let us put together the strongest possible argument in favor of the proposal that "radar detectors should be outlawed," and then proceed to scrutinize that argument critically to see whether or not it appears to be based upon a firm, nonrelative foundation. I have not as yet developed the procedures to do this thoroughly, but we can use common sense and imagination; the key is whether or not the support for the claim should appeal to anybody regardless of his or her personal or cultural bias.

In the present case, then, we might encounter the following argument as support for the claim: Radar detectors should be outlawed because their users tend to drive at higher speeds than they would otherwise and therefore run a greater risk of serious injury and even death. The greater speeds also endanger others on the highway. In addition, lower speeds have been shown to save fuel (a finite, nonrenewable energy resource) and to reduce air pollution.

Let us list these items separately:

1. Drivers using radar detectors tend to drive faster than they would otherwise.
2. Therefore, the use of radar detectors contributes to greater risk of serious injury and death [than their nonuse would].
3. Lower speeds conserve fuel, which is a finite, nonrenewable energy resource.
4. Lower speeds reduce air pollution.

If we pursued the matter further, we might find that the second statement (involving the increased risk of serious injury and death) can be substantiated by reliable highway department statistics that correlate with the commonsense view that slower speeds are safer. The first statement supports the second and is clearly a reason for the second statement. It claims—although this point is difficult to establish from a logical point of view—that cars using radar detectors do, in fact, travel at higher speeds than they would without the detectors. This is a factual consideration and would, if true, appear to strengthen the second statement.

The third and fourth statements can be shown to be strong on empirical grounds because higher speeds do tend (generally) to burn more fuel and produce more air pollution. If we attach an ethical principle (to be defended in the next chapter) to the effect that we should adopt ethical rules that increase human happiness, the conclusion that radar detectors should be outlawed appears to be quite strong. This is because the number of people made unhappy by the outlawing of detectors is small in comparison with the number of people who would be made happy by increased safety and cleaner air.

We therefore need to add a fifth statement to the list:

5. [P] One should adopt rules that increase the happiness of those affected by the rules.

For the purpose of this particular argument, we will need to add another premise. This premise is an assumption.

6. [A] In this instance laws should be made to enforce ethical rules.

I note in passing that, generally speaking, the assumption that laws should be made to enforce *every* ethical rule is implausible. Because of the social consequences of the use of radar detectors, however, the assumption seems warranted in this case. But this is something you should consider carefully, as assumptions are frequently the heart and soul of an argument. The fact that they are usually unstated is all the more reason to ferret them out and think about them seriously, as we shall see in Chapter Three.

We seem, however, to be confronted by a strong argument—one that *should* appeal to every reasonable person, including users of radar detectors. That is, the facts adduced to support the claim do not appear to be merely "relative." Furthermore, they seem to be able to withstand critical scrutiny, since for the most part they are collected by disinterested groups and are generally accessible. Whether or not this is true in the case of the ethical principle we shall see in the next chapter. But it certainly appears to be so in the case of the evidence provided: It is difficult to see how this evidence could be dismissed as "cultural bias." The only weakness in the argument, as I have pointed out in passing, is the claim that drivers using detectors drive faster than they would if they did not use detectors (statement 1). This is what logicians call a "counter-to-fact conditional" and cannot, strictly speaking, be verified. How can we know, in this case, that the same people would drive slower than they do under different circumstances? Common sense suggests that this is the case, but it is a weaker claim than statements 2, 3, and 4, which are based on empirical data.

In order to strengthen the argument further, we might show awareness of other points of view (some of which are strongly held) and critically consider counter-arguments—knowing full well that if we weaken a counter-argument we strengthen our own. We might, for example, argue against the view, sometimes held, that laws against radar detectors limit the freedom of citizens who might wish to buy and use them, or, as the "Doonesbury" cartoon suggests, that their use is a form of "libertarian civil disobedience."

Unfortunately, the student in Trudeau's cartoon presents a weak argument because it rests on the emotional appeal of the word "freedom" (which makes it fallacious, as we shall see in Chapter Three). It ignores the fact that in a free society all citizens are not free to

do whatever they like if what they like to do harms other members of their community. Laws also limit the freedom of citizens to set off hand grenades in crowded squares, yet we approve the fact that these laws limit the freedom of would-be terrorists. To a lesser degree, this would appear to be the case with radar detectors.

It is true, of course, that outlawing radar detectors does limit one's freedom. But if the argument given here is strong—as it appears to be—there would seem to be good grounds for limiting that freedom, since use of the detectors has serious social consequences that will decrease human happiness.

The claim that radar detectors should be outlawed would seem to be well argued and therefore acceptable to anybody capable of following the argument. Unless some claims have been ignored that should be considered, it would seem that we have an example of a nonrelative ethical claim.

Nonrelative Ethical Claims

I contend that arguments incorporating nonrelative claims—that is, claims that can withstand criticism and scrutiny and appear to involve few, if any, relative factors—are binding on all rational persons regardless of cultural upbringing and personal preference. And this includes ethical arguments. A strong ethical argument, in a word, is one that should be accepted by anybody who considers it carefully, whether or not he or she *wants* to accept it. This is a very controversial claim. Do you accept it?

In any event, I must note that there is much remaining to be done to establish this thesis. Perhaps if you are still unconvinced, your mind will change in the face of stronger arguments yet to come. We shall see. I must yet examine thoroughly the process of justification whereby ethical conclusions pass the test of critical scrutiny. We need to arm ourselves with some basic techniques of critical reasoning that will enable us to examine ethical arguments—our own as well as those put forth by others. It might also be helpful if we consider carefully what is distinctive about *ethical* reasoning. But our first order of business is to continue our defense of nonrelativism with a look at how it is possible to reduce or eliminate personal and cultural prejudice from ethical judgments in order to make ethical claims stronger.

1.3 HOW OBJECTIVE CAN WE BE?

My present object is to defend the possibility of justifiable, cross-cultural judgments in ethics against the view of the relativist that these judgments are always and invariably personal or cultural. The defense will continue by addressing some of the views put forward by the cultural relativist that appear at first glance to be plausible.

For one thing, must we not admit, as the relativist contends, that our ethical claims are unavoidably saturated with personal and cultural bias? Yes and no. Ethical claims do involve personal and cultural bias in many, if not all, cases. However, as I said earlier, we are capable of reducing or eliminating personal and cultural bias in our truth claims—in ethics just as we do in science and the social sciences. As a result, these claims can reach a level of objectivity that the relativist refuses to allow. I shall try to show this in some detail in the present section by showing that we do not doubt the objectivity of science, despite the fact that personal and cultural biases often enter into scientific claims.

Eliminating Prejudice in Science

Let us look at the way science attempts to dislodge prejudice and establish new theories in order to (1) see how this happens and (2) see whether or not there are lessons there to help us in ethical reasoning.

In 1923 Louis de Broglie proposed to several members of the scientific "establishment," including Paul Langevin and Charles Mauguin, the thesis that particles in motion have wave properties. The theory appealed to de Broglie, he tells us, because of its intellectual elegance and beauty, although the view was at odds with theories generally accepted at the time. The group of professors to whom the theory was suggested didn't know quite what to make of it and asked Albert Einstein for advice. Einstein immediately recognized the possibilities of the new theory and recommended that de Broglie's thesis be accepted. Mauguin later recalled that

> when the thesis was presented I did not believe in the physical reality of the waves associated with the particles of matter. I saw in them, rather, pure creations of the mind. . . . Only after the experiments of Davisson and German [in 1927], of G.P. Thompson [in 1928],

and only when I held in my hand the beautiful photographs [of electron diffraction patterns from the layers of zinc oxide], which Ponte had succeeded in making in the Ecole Normale, did I understand how inconsistent, ridiculous, and nonsensical my attitude was.[11]

The same reluctance to accept a new theory hounded the Copernican view we discussed in the last section. After all, as we saw, the Ptolemaic theory accorded with common sense: We still talk about the sun "rising" and "setting." Furthermore, it placed human beings at the center of the universe; it was consistent with Aristotelian natural philosophy, which was officially recognized and accepted by the Roman Catholic Church; it was a view that had persisted for over seventeen hundred years; and it allowed for fairly accurate prediction of lunar eclipses and was, in its day, mathematically sophisticated. Additionally, it required that planets travel in perfect circular motion, which accorded with the general understanding of God's design. The new view, in contrast, required that the earth move through space at great speed in elliptical orbits—or "quasicircles" as Copernicus called them until Kepler later identified them as ellipses. This did *not* accord with common sense or Church doctrine. However, as the evidence mounted it became increasingly clear than many of the preconceptions and convictions based on the Ptolemaic view were (at best) half truths or (at worst) totally unacceptable. As we saw, new mathematical methods, new discoveries in mechanics, and increasingly accurate measurements made possible by the invention and use of the telescope led thinkers such as Copernicus to feel "the real necessity of substituting for the complicated Ptolemaic system some other hypothesis that would better agree with the observations, steadily growing more numerous and more accurate."[12] Some of the claims, such as the view that planets travel in perfect circular motion, were simply beliefs supported by little more than a strong desire that the belief be true, rather than by any rational evidence. Recall that Copernicus, too, was convinced that the heavenly planets must travel in circular (or "quasi-circular") orbits—so strong was this prejudice. It took a great deal of time to move this mass of conviction and displace it with the more accurate and reasonable heliocentric view. One thing that caused delay and confused even the most astute thinkers of the day was the relationship between astrology and astronomy. Kepler, for example, writing ninety years after Copernicus first proposed his view, evidenced in his writings an odd blend of astrology and astronomy, and a bit of ancient Pythagorean religious philosophy as well. He

> believed that the ratios between the maximum and minimum velocities of the planets along their orbits should be harmonic in a musical sense. Thus, for instance, he found for Saturn the major third (4/5) for Jupiter a minor third (5/6) and so on. Only the sun could hear the celestial music.[13]

It wasn't until Newton's *Principia* that the heliocentric view began to clear itself of its astrological trappings—and that book appeared over 150 years after Copernicus first proposed his theory in 1530! Such was the weight of prejudice and tradition that accompanied the Ptolemaic view.

A Contemporary Example: Creationism

You might think from these examples that science has finally reached a point where prejudice no longer plays a role. This is almost certainly false. One of the most provocative controversies on the current scene is the debate over creationism and the question of whether or not it should be taught in the schools as another scientific perspective. The interesting thing about this example is that some would claim the scientific community is prejudiced against the creationist theory—in much the same way the Church was prejudiced against the Copernican theory centuries ago!

There are several versions of creationism, from the most conservative, "young earth" creationists who espouse a literal interpretation of the Bible and insist that the world was created between six thousand and ten thousand years ago, to the more progressive creationists who try to adapt the Bible to contemporary science. The conservative view has made little, if any, headway in making its case to be included in school curricula as a strictly scientific perspective. But the more moderate view has a stronger case and raises some interesting questions. This end of the creationist spectrum is made up of people who are are sometimes referred to as "theistic evolutionists"; they maintain that "evolution is part of God's plan" and that the world shows signs of "intelligent design" that cannot be accounted for in the strictly Darwinian view of evolution. For the most part, the "intelligent-design" camp points to gaps in Darwinian theory and insists that evolution cannot be simply a matter of random factors that we explain away with the term "coincidence." Members of this group make a clear distinction "between 'microevolution,' with which they are comfortable (because this process provides only for variation within species, such as moths developing darker wings for camouflage in response to pollution) and 'macroevolution,' which is counter to their beliefs because such a process requires 'major innovations' in speciation that occurs naturalistically, without the guidance of a creator."[14]

The reason that the more moderate version of creationism (whose advocates rarely refer to themselves as "creationists") is interesting and worthy of note is that it is peopled by a number of respectible professionals, including scientists, who do not reject Darwinism but who insist that the notion of "intelligent design" should be taught along with Darwinism, that creationism and Darwinism can be made compatible. In a word, they seek a compromise of sorts and insist that the refusal to talk about God in connection with the creation of the world and the origin of species is little more than a prejudice. What do you think?

Progress in Science—and Ethics

There are two considerations that arise from this discussion that are of chief interest to us: First, new views must work against the great inertial force of fixed opinion, preconceptions, and predispositions that are a blend of truths, comforting half-truths, falsehoods, deceptions, wishful thinking, and outright prejudice. Second, the new views do, occasionally, succeed in replacing the older views, and the faulty and the weak support that had sustained them is recognized as inadequate. In this sense, there is what we call "scientific progress."

Similarly, it makes perfectly good sense to speak about ethical progress. Just as it is no longer possible to (reasonably) insist that planets travel in circular motion, so also it is no longer possible to reasonably claim that blacks are inferior to whites, or that women are less intelligent or less able than men. The notion of "universal suffrage" no longer includes only propertied white males—as it did in past centuries—but includes all persons. We no longer have *autos-da-fe* where heretics are publicly burned; nor do we have witch-hunts or Inquisitions. We have advanced to the point in ethics that certain claims have revealed themselves as nothing more than blatant prejudice. Other biases are less obvious, but it is possible to recognize them nonetheless. Ridding ourselves of them once they have been discovered may be rather difficult, but it can be done. Mistakes can be made in our ethical judgments, and it is possible to recognize those mistakes and correct them. This point was driven home recently in a comment made by the majority opinion of the Supreme Court in their decision dealing with sex between homosexuals. They said, in part, that "the court's support of anti-sodomy laws seventeen years ago was not correct when it was decided, and it is not correct today." Often, as in this case, what blocked correct judgment was strong homophobic prejudice—even in the highest court in the land!

If we find ourselves supporting ethical claims with platitudes and half-truths that "we have always heard" or make us feel "comfortable" but for which we can find no rational support, or if we reject something because we find it "disgusting" or because "that sort of thing just isn't done"—but we can't say *why*—we are probably dealing with prejudice—or ignorance, at best. This does not mean that if we cannot explain why we hold onto the convictions we happen to embrace, those convictions must be falsehoods or prejudices. It means that if we cannot say why we hold these convictions we need to scrutinize them carefully for signs of prejudice and try to determine whether or not they are capable of being supported by evidence and argument. If we cannot find any argument or evidence to support them, the likelihood that they are prejudices increases.

Prejudice is embodied in a set of convictions we cling to because we are disinclined to examine them—for one reason or another. The term is variously defined, but the psychologist Gordon Allport quotes with approval the definition of prejudice as "a judgment formed before due examination and consideration of the facts—a premature or hasty judgment."[15] While strong feelings are often attached to prejudices, they always involve a "prejudgment" that is frequently based on familiarity or long-held beliefs for which we have insufficient evidence. However, something is not true simply because we have always believed it to be true, and if our innermost convictions and beliefs are not worthy of acceptance, then they should be replaced by others that are.

Relativism is unacceptable from a philosophical point of view because it is based on oversimplification. Admittedly prejudice enters into our ethical judgments. But it does not follow that *therefore* those judgments are nothing more than a bundle of prejudices. As we have seen, we can recognize and at least partially eliminate prejudice; and we can insist upon support for our claims that is binding upon all reasonable people of good willl—that is, people who are willing to keep an open mind and admit that they might be wrong. Thus, while there is an element of truth in the relativist's position, we must not mistake it for the whole truth.

Cross-Cultural Judgments in Ethics

Before leaving this section, I must attend to one other element of truth in the relativist's position. I have admitted that ethical judgments are strongly influenced—although not determined—by our personal or cultural perspective. I now must also admit that cross-cultural judgments in ethics are difficult to justify. That is, ethical judgments made within one culture about activities taking place in another culture are, admittedly, problematic. As anthropologists have argued for more than a century, no one outside a particular culture can ever totally share the cultural perspective of those raised within that culture. Every culture possesses a language that is rich with tradition and layered with emotional meaning, or "connotation," that can only be grasped by those who have been raised within that culture and who have used that language from birth. In addition, there are practices, both regular and occasional, that cannot be explained to foreigners. At best, persons outside that culture can only hope to witness and enjoy these practices; they cannot ever expect to fully appreciate, much less understand, them.

Given that this is so, I must acknowledge that much of what is happening within a culture other than my own (or a subculture within my own culture) is beyond my ken. This does not mean, however, that *everything* that happens within another culture must remain opaque to outsiders and that judgments can *never* cross cultural boundaries. Once again, we must be wary of mistaking a half-truth for the whole truth.

Far too much has been made of cultural differences since anthropologists began to catalogue them in the late eighteenth century. To be sure, there are a great many differences. Furthermore, following the lead of most anthropologists, we do want to avoid "ethnocentrism," or the view that other cultures, being different from ours, are somehow "inferior" to ours: There is no reason to allow that any culture is "superior" or "inferior" to any other culture, *as a culture*. Indeed, this is an absurd claim. It may be possible to argue, however, that certain cultural *practices* are superior or inferior to others. In saying this I hasten to add that criticism cuts both ways: It is not applicable only to other cultures; some of the things we do in our culture may well be worthy of criticism and condemnation from another cultural perspective—and that perspective may very well be clearer and more accurate than our own!

The nonrelativist does not presume that his or her cultural perspective is superior to all others, nor does he or she insist that any one cultural perspective is somehow *the* correct perspective. What nonrelativism maintains is that if persons within two different cultures utter conflicting ethical judgments, they may both be wrong but *they cannot both be correct*. The view also maintains that it is sometimes possible, and philosophically interesting, to resolve intercultural differences reasonably.

It is, of course, quite difficult to say in a particular case which of two conflicting views is the "correct" view. But we can reach reasonable conclusions in this regard. We must work through our own biases into another cultural perspective—as far as possible. And we know it can be done, because it is done almost daily.

Consider: Cultural perspectives are shared when literature written by members of one culture delights or terrifies members of another culture; it happens whenever communication takes place between men and women, blacks and whites, native people and nonnative people; it also happens whenever people raised in one culture perform music composed in another culture, and do so with sensitivity and insight. It is commonplace that "something is lost in translation," but we must hasten to add that something is also discovered!

Cross-Cultural Judgments—An Example or Two

Although much of what people in another culture say remains "untranslatable," not all of it is. We can gain an adequate understanding and appreciation of what goes on in another culture, and at times we reason correctly that something is wrong. Let us take an example—one not unlike the case that disturbed Nina in the opening dialogue—to make our case.

We know that Spartans in the fourth and fifth centuries B.C. abandoned weak or deformed infants in a chasm under Taygetus. We have a pretty good idea why the Spartans did this: They did it to purge the race of persons unfit to serve the *polis*—an idea Plato found appealing. Plutarch put it rather graphically in describing the motives of the elders of the tribe:

> . . . as thinking it neither for the good of the child itself, nor for the public interest, that it should be brought up, if it did not, from the very outset, appear made to be healthy and vigorous.[16]

Even though we cannot fully understand why the Spartans felt it necessary to do this, since we are not ourselves Spartans, we can understand it well enough to say that as a practice it is rationally indefensible. There are at least two compelling reasons why the Spartans should not have engaged in this practice:

1. Physical ability is not the only (or even the most important) measure of a person's value to society. The Spartans, being a bellicose people who found it necessary to practice the art of war daily, placed great emphasis on physical strength and prowess. As a result, they overlooked the ways their society might have benefitted from the nonmilitary contributions of "disabled" people. This is a factual consideration that involves few, if any, "value" judgments. As such, it should appeal to persons brought up in any culture—even Spartans.

2. Infanticide is a blatant violation of the right all persons have to life; therefore (as we shall see) what the Spartans did was ethically wrong. In this regard, Nina was perfectly correct to object to the practice in Achebe's fictional village. And this is so whether or not the Spartans, or the Umuofians, themselves recognized the rights of twins or physically handicapped persons. We need not develop an argument to defend this claim; we need only consider that the Spartans' defense of infanticide was based on a prejudice that did not allow them to see the potential value to the Spartan *polis* of persons who are merely physically inhibited, while the Umuofian's rationale was based on superstition, which is without rational base. Thus, even without stating any reasons to support the view that the Spartans or Umuofians were wrong, using the method of critical rationalism, we can show that the reasons *they* gave in support of the practice do not withstand scrutiny. If that is so, and you should think about this carefully, then whatever case we might make for the Spartans and the Umuofians being wrong in engaging in infanticide is made considerably stronger. If they cannot rationally defend their practice, this lends credence to the opposite view.

A second, more contemporary, example might help to make quite clear what the disagreement is between the relativist and the nonrelativist—if any confusion still remains.

Consider the case of the group of militant Muslims who took over several airliners and flew them into the Twin Towers and the Pentagon on September 11, 2001. The world was horrified at this act of brutality, but the terrorists themselves saw it as an expression of their religious conviction. They were regarded by their fellow militants as martyrs who died a hero's death in a divine cause. The relativist would say: Who are we to judge whether what these men did was right or wrong? We are not of their culture and we have never walked "a mile in their shoes." We may not like what they did, we may find it deplorable, but we are not in a position to make any ethical judgments one way or the other.

The nonrelativist, on the other hand, would respond that these (and other) acts of terrorism are clearly wrong: They violate the basic right every human has to life, and, if challenged, the nonrelativist would be able to support this claim with an argument. That argument would involve a basic ethical principle—which we shall examine in the next chapter. But it would claim to be binding on anyone capable of following the argument, including the terrorists themselves. A recent comment by someone who has reflected on this issue a great deal may, in the end, be correct. He said that "thinkers increasingly agree that relativism is a position that has played an important historical role but is difficult now to sustain." And he quotes thinkers from other cultures to support his position. "Human rights," as was noted by Bilahari Kausikan of Singapore (a non-Westerner, please note), "have become a legitimate issue in interstate relations. How a country treats its citizens [or noncitizens] is no longer a matter for its own exclusive determination." This claim was seconded by Japan's leading human rights expert, Yasuaki Onuma, who insisted that "there is increasing recognition that 'states can no longer conveniently deny the universality of human rights.' "[17] I shall examine the notion of "human rights" closely in the next chapter (and

I shall also examine, in the third chapter, the question of whether or not quoting someone in authority is a persuasive reason to support a point of view!).

Food for Further Thought

A philosophy instructor once made the statement in a class that Albert Schweitzer was a better man than Hitler. Now, aside from the fact that no one in that class knew who Albert Schweitzer was (he was a medical doctor and an organist of considerable talent and ability who turned his back on fame and fortune in Germany to treat poor natives in Africa), it appeared to the instructor that this was a statement everyone would accept. Not so! Several students in the class were outraged that anyone would go so far as to say that one human being was better (or worse) than another. It was noted that to a room full of skinhead neo-Nazis that claim would be roundly denounced because all in the room would insist that Hitler was the better man. This objection is excellent and raises a good point: What do we do if some, or all, who weigh the "rational support" for the claims we make *reject* that support? This can happen: It probably would happen in a room full of neo-Nazis! But, the question to ponder is whether or not this weakens the case for nonrelativism. Consider an analogy. Suppose a room filled with flat earth advocates were listening to a lecture on the solar system. Do you think there would be any converts to the Newtonian view? Can we dismiss the neo-Nazis and the flat earth members as mere fanatics with closed minds? Or must we admit, in the end, that it is all relative?

It is tempting to dismiss anyone who disagrees with us as one who is blinded by prejudice—but is this merely a cop-out? Is prejudice, as suggested, always with us and something we must simply deal with? Or can we rise above it, as suggested in the text, by becoming aware of it?

On the face of it, most of what happens in another culture is alien to us and subject to neither praise nor blame for that reason. But occasionally what happens "there" is wrong and for that reason is worthy of condemnation. In some serious cases, it might be argued, the wrong requires condemnation and possible intervention.

The word "condemn" bothers us, however, and rightly so. The word smacks of authoritarianism and intolerance, of invasions by armies or, at the very least, by missionaries. But tolerance, as mentioned earlier, may not always be ethically desirable—as when on-lookers ignore the frantic cries of a rape victim. Furthermore, it may be nothing more than another word for "indifference," which is hardly laudable from an ethical point of view. But I need not take the argument that far. At present, I am only interested in the philosophical basis for condemnation and praise, and I am simply saying that cultural boundaries are not insurmountable in every case. Or are they? What do you think?

My argument suggests that we can admit much of what the cultural relativist claims about the nature of prejudice and the difficulties of avoiding cultural bias, without drawing the same conclusions. Despite the fact that we are all products of "enculturation," we can come close to understanding other cultural perspectives and appreciate the reasons why people do as they do. We need not accept the conclusion that what they do is "therefore" (invariably) right because it cannot be accurately judged from the perspective of another culture. We can also admit that we must sometimes operate in ethics through a thick mist of prejudice without accepting the conclusion that the mist cannot occasionally be reduced or penetrated by the light of reason. But is it merely a dodge to insist that those who disagree with us are being "unreasonable" and are simply blinded by prejudice? How does one decide what is and what is not "reasonable"?

In the end, there appear to be a number of ways to cross cultural boundaries, intellectually, and to reduce or remove our personal and cultural prejudices. One way is to increase our sensitivity to prejudice in its many guises; another way is to improve our critical skills so that we can recognize and appreciate strong ethical arguments that cut through the mist of bias and prejudice and transcend cultural boundaries; and, finally, we can see more clearly how ethical conflict is generated and how it might be resolved by adopting an "ethical perspective," which provides us with a broader and more distanced point of view. Consider, for example, how much easier it is to think clearly about a problem that does not involve us directly—say, one that involves persons, like the Spartans, we never knew because they lived in another time and place. This is significant, and it gives us a clue about what the ethical perspective involves. Establishing this perspective will be my goal in the next chapter. Later chapters will deal with methods necessary for the analysis and evaluation of ethical arguments. We will see if these considerations can help us to answer some of the nagging questions just raised.

NOTES

1. Philip Davis and Ruben Hersh, *Descartes' Dream,* Boston: Houghton Mifflin, 1986, p. 207.
2. *Ibid.,* p. 213.
3. Nancy Gifford, *When in Rome.* New York: State University Press, 1983, p. 28.
4. Terry Eagleton, *The Illusions of Postmodernism,* Blackwell, 1996, Malden, Mass.: p. 27.
5. Gifford, *When in Rome,* p. 77.
6. Giorgio Abetti, *The History of Astronomy,* London: Abelard Schuman, 1952 (Tr. Betty Abetti), p. 75.
7. Karl Popper, *Conjectures and Refutations,* New York: Harper and Row, 1965, p. 25.
8. Raphael Sealey, *A History of the Greek City States,* Berkeley: University of California Press, 1976, p. 29.
9. Malcolm Todd, *Everyday Life of the Barbarians,* New York: Dorset Press, 1972, p. 5.
10. *Ibid.,* p. 253.
11. *Louis de Broglie und die Physiker,* quoted in Michael Polany, *Personal Knowledge,* Chicago: University of Chicago Press, 1962, p. 148, n.1.
12. Abetti, *The History of Astronomy,* p. 72.
13. *Ibid.,* p. 120.
14. Amy J. Binder, *Contentious Curricula.* Princeton, N.J.: Princeton University Press, 2002, p. 41.
15. Gordon Allport, *The Nature of Prejudice,* Boston: Beacon Press, 1954, p. 7.
16. Plutarch, *Lives of the Noble Grecians and Romans,* New York: Modern Library, (Tr. John Dryden), p. 62.
17. References here are from Amatai Etzioni, *The Monochrome Society,* Princeton, N.J.: Princeton University Press, 2001, pp. 232, 233.

CHAPTER TWO

The Framework

2.1 RESPECT, FAIRNESS, AND HUMAN HAPPINESS: THREE TRADITIONAL PRINCIPLES IN ETHICAL ARGUMENTS

Our word "ethics" is from the Greek *ēthikós*, which is a variant of *ēthos* meaning "custom" or, more accurately, "that which is done." Even in ancient Athens there was considerable disagreement about whether the "is" referred to what is *actually* done—as in "Einert picks his teeth after every meal"—or what is *ideally* done—as in "Einert, you shouldn't pick your teeth in public; it just isn't done!"

If Plato is to be believed, the sophists in Athens insisted on the former interpretation and became staunch defenders of what we have labelled "relativism." They viewed ethics as a *descriptive* study that notes and catalogues the things people do, as a matter of fact. Socrates, and later Plato and then Aristotle, disagreed, insisting that ethics is *normative,* a careful and systematic investigation of the things people *should* do—regardless of cultural bias or what is considered "normal" behavior.

In the ten books of *The Nicomachean Ethics*, for example, Aristotle painstakingly analyzed the concept of *areté*—which is usually translated as "virtue," but which means considerably more than we do when we use that word. *Areté* has to do with human excellence, and includes both strong character (moral virtue, according to Aristotle) and intelligence (intellectual virtue). Of central importance in Aristotle's analysis was membership in a human community, which for Aristotle, as for most Greeks, meant membership in the *polis*, or city-state. His pivotal point, and one of considerable interest to us at the moment, was that *only* through membership in a larger human community can persons achieve self-actualization, become fully human. Membership in a community produces language, thought, laws, and culture, including manners, which are those factors that enable the community to maintain itself and the person to become happy.

Human Happiness as an Ideal

Aristotle's notion of happiness is intriguing. When he talks about happiness, Aristotle does not mean what we usually mean by the word; he is not talking about giddy feelings—about those things that give us pleasure. He is not saying what Snoopy says when he tells us that "happiness is a cold nose," or what your friend Pete says when he tells you that "happiness is in the bottle drunk." Happiness, for Aristotle, is a normative concept: It refers to those things that *ought* to make humans happy. Furthermore, happiness in this sense is not a momentary thing, like the bottle drunk or the cold nose. It is a human condition that encompasses an entire lifetime. One cannot be happy here and now; one can claim to be happy only if he or she has lived a full and virtuous life.

Aristotle ties together his notion of virtue, or human excellence, with happiness. The virtuous person is happy and vice versa. We become happy, in our lifetime, by making correct choices about what will in fact make us more human. These correct choices are the result of good character combined with good judgment. As children our parents (and the city) help us to develop the habits of virtue—what we would call "character," such things as honesty, self-control, concern for others, and the like. As we grow older, we need to develop "practical wisdom," or prudence, to help us choose the correct means to those ends that will make us more human.

Is Happiness a "Dated" Notion?

All of this might sound a bit old-fashioned to the modern ear. But it is not when we translate it into today's vernacular. Aristotle is saying that good men and women are what men and women *ought* to be. They do the things that you and I wish we had done: We admire them. Clearly Aristotle has a paradigm in mind, perhaps Socrates. There is an ideal of human nature toward which we ought to direct our activity, and this ideal is the same for all of us. This notion strikes us as peculiar because we have been raised to revere individuality as our ideal. But Aristotle does not rule out differences or insist that everyone be like everyone else: He merely says that everyone should be measured against the same paradigm, since human nature is one and unchanging—the same now as it was in Aristotle's day. Some people, he would say, are better than other people; they more nearly approximate that ideal of human nature: Albert Schweitzer was a better man than Hitler, for example. Most of us would agree with this (in our unguarded moments, at least) and tend to measure ourselves and others against some sort of vague notion about "what people ought to do." Aristotle would simply have us develop this notion more carefully and more clearly. In doing this himself, he arrived at his notion of "virtue," which is the human good toward which all human activity ought to be directed and in terms of which all human behavior ought to be judged. As individuals we realize that ideal, or fail to realize it, in accordance with our individual capabilities and in accordance with luck, or good fortune, both of which are different for every person. If a person directs his or her life toward the highest human good, or virtue, and is fortunate enough to have such things as good friends and wealth enough to keep the wolf from the door, then at the end of that person's life we can say with some confidence that he or she was "happy."

The interesting thing about Aristotle's ethics is that it has recently enjoyed a resurgence in the form of what is called "virtue ethics." One of the most popular versions of this particular view is "the ethics of care," which has been developed by a number of, especially, feminist philosophers who think that the approach I will take in this chapter is too narrow in its exclusive focus on ethical principles. The ethics of care and virtue ethics tend to play down the importance of principles and stress the nature of the person who acts: A virtuous person, a person who cares about other people, will do the right thing. In the view of these thinkers, it's not a question of applying principles to specific actions; it is a matter of being a good person, one who cares about others, and about doing the right thing as a consequence of character.

There is a great strength in these positions, and I will have more to say about them later in this chapter. In the meantime, I will continue to develop a case for three ethical principles that I consider central to ethical thinking. And one of the things that is particularly important and valuable in Aristotle's ethics is his notion of the central place of the human community in ethics. This is a notion that has become increasingly important in both virtue ethics and the ethics of care. Let us explore this notion briefly.

The Human Community

Community membership involves subordination of the individual to the community of which he or she is a part—in much the same way a member of an athletic team subordinates himself or herself to the goals of the team. Subordination involves self-sacrifice but not self-denial, since membership for the individual in the community involves many more benefits than costs. Recall that for Aristotle community membership is necessary for persons to achieve their *human* potential. Exclusion from the human community, from the city-state, was anathema to the Greeks and may have been one of the reasons why Socrates chose death rather that exile from Athens.

In the community, then, the individual learns that what benefits all benefits each, and that apart from others each of us is less than human. This is the central idea behind Aristotle's ethics, generally. Membership in the human community requires a set of expectations, or norms, of interpersonal behavior. In the years since Aristotle, these norms have evolved into certain principles that have been articulated (in one form or another) by various philosophers in an attempt to produce a coherent and integrated view of what membership in the human community involves.

The view presented in this book closely follows Socrates, Plato, and Aristotle in regarding ethics as normative rather than descriptive—as concerned with how we ought to behave rather than how we do behave as a matter of fact. In the ideal human community persons would respect one another as persons, or moral agents, and treat each other with fairness. Additionally, if they formulated rules to govern interpersonal activity, those rules would increase human happiness (in Aristotle's sense of that term). These are the principles I shall develop and defend in this chapter.

Three Central Ethical Principles

Three principles encapsulate the most basic conditions that make ethical reasoning and, indeed, ethics itself possible. They focus attention on respect for persons, fairness, and consequences and can be stated as follows:

---

1. Treat the person in yourself and others with respect.
2. Treat all persons fairly.
3. Consistent with 1 and 2, adopt a rule for action that will increase the happiness of a majority of those affected by the rule.

Principle #1: Respect for Persons

The first principle owes its origin to the German philosopher Immanuel Kant, who has already been mentioned. For some, Kant's ethical view is sufficient without the addition of other principles. But for most critics, problems result from Kant's view which necessitate the other two principles.

Kant calls moral persons "ends in themselves." The phrase stresses the importance of *respect* for persons, the cornerstone of Kant's ethical philosophy. Kant insists that we should respect moral persons and not "treat them merely as a means" to another end because they are moral agents, that is, they have the capacity to act morally. That is, we ought not to use other persons for our purposes—whatever those purposes happen to be. Kant's concern for persons is primarily *negative*, leading to a series of proscriptions and leaving some room for doubt about what positive measures we should take in dealing with one another. He stresses the obligation *not* to treat persons as means, *not* to use other persons (or oneself), *not* to coerce persons, and the like. To be sure, he argues that we should promote the happiness of other persons and work to realize our own capabilities as much as possible. But while these admonitions add positive dimensions to the concept of respect for oneself and others, it is not clear how they follow from Kant's prior declaration that we treat ourselves and others as ends. This is another reason why I have augmented Kant's concept of respect for persons with two further principles.

The importance of Kant's notion of respect for persons cannot be stressed too much; indeed, I propose that it is a *necessary* condition for any ethical action. That means that if we do not respect persons, or if we act in such a way as to violate the principle of respect for persons, then we cannot claim that our action has ethical worth.

PERSONS HAVE RIGHTS. If we all have an obligation to respect the person in ourselves and in others, then all persons have the *right* to be respected as persons. This is so because rights, as a rule, imply correlative responsibilities, or obligations. If Barbara has a right to be treated with respect, so do all other persons, and Barbara, like everybody else, ought to respect those rights if she expects hers to be respected. Barbara's right is a natural, or human, right, and it is attributable to persons simply by virtue of the fact that they are persons: They don't do anything to earn it. As Kant would have it, persons are different from non-persons (things) in that they not only follow desire and instinct, but they also have the capacity (whether or not they exercise it) to formulate, and are free to obey or disobey, moral laws. This capacity is central to what it means to be a person, and ignoring it constitutes a serious breach of the duty we all have to respect one another—such mutual respect being the bedrock of ethical behavior for Kant.

If we all have rights simply by virtue of being persons, however, is it not possible to *forfeit* those rights? That is to say, granted that we do not earn these rights and no one else can take them away from us—as Thomas Jefferson said, they are inalienable—can we not forfeit them *ourselves* by refusing to exercise our capacity to act morally? Can we not forfeit our right to be respected by others if, say, we commit a capital crime? Kant certainly thought this could happen.

CAN RIGHTS BE FORFEITED? In one of his *Lectures on Ethics,* Kant makes the point that

> We may have lost everything else and yet still retain our inherent worth. Only if our worth as human beings is intact can we perform our other duties; for it is the foundation stone of all other duties. A man who has destroyed and cast away his personality, has no intrinsic worth, and can no longer perform any manner of duty.[1]

The word "forfeiture" is not mentioned, of course, but clearly this is what the phrase "cast away his personality" means. The idea was not original with Kant, however, but can be found in the writings of Saint Thomas Aquinas some six hundred years earlier. Aquinas tells us that

> By sinning a man falls back from the level of reason, and to that extent loses the dignity of a human person free within and existing in his own right. He falls into the slavish condition of the beasts, so that he can be disposed of and treated as a utility. . . . Hence, though it is intrinsically wicked to kill a man who has kept his worth, nevertheless it may be right to put a criminal out of the way, as it is to kill an animal. Indeed, an evil man is worse than a beast and more harmful, as Aristotle says.[2]

As we can plainly see, Kant is writing within an established tradition. His words, echoing his predecessor, seem so calm and assured, straightforward and uncompromising. Unfortunately, it was not that easy. No sooner were the words quoted here written down than he seemed to have second thoughts. In a later essay, "Duties Toward Others," Kant seems to renege on his earlier position. He says that

> If a man be a rogue, I disapprove of him as a man, but however wicked he is there is still some core of good will in him, and if I distinguish between his humanity and the man himself I can contemplate even the rougue with pleasure. . . .

> No rogue is so abandoned that he does not appreciate the difference between good and bad and does not wish to be virtuous.[3]

Kant's lack of consistency here suggests that there are problems with the idea of forfeiture of rights. These problems lead me to reject the notion of forfeiture, even though that rejection results in some perplexing difficulties to be touched on later.

RIGHTS CANNOT BE FORFEITED. The first problem with the concept of forfeiture of rights lies in the following question: "*When* does one forfeit those rights?" What constitutes a serious enough breach of respect for others to warrant the loss of one's "personhood," one's right to be respected by others? If a man charges through the door waving a pistol and demanding all my money, can I take the poker next to the fireplace and crush his skull with impunity? Or does he have to actually take possession of my money? Or does he have to point the pistol at me and threaten to shoot?

He hasn't fired the pistol at this point and, indeed, it could be un-loaded or a toy and he might have been put up to this charade by some friends of mine as a practical joke. (I have some strange friends!) Or does the man forfeit his right to be treated as a person when he has fired the pistol and killed someone? Or does he for-feit it later, when the jury finds him guilty? But what if the jury makes a mistake? He is seen leaving the scene of the crime with a smoking gun in his hand, but someone else is mistaken for him and that person is subsequently tried and convicted of the murder and summarily executed. If we discover that this happened we might say, "Gee, I'm sorry! It seems we made a mistake!" Mistakes happen and every day innocent people are found guilty of crimes they didn't commit. I ask again: When, exactly, does forfeiture happen?

The second problem is whether or not forfeiture is final. This seems to be the question Kant was struggling with in the second passage quoted earlier. Is it right to take other people's lives when they have forfeited their right to be respected as persons because of, let us say, a criminal act about which there can be no doubt? Or is it possible that by virtue of some future act they could redeem them-selves twice over? Suppose, as the Russian novelist Dostoevsky did while writing *Crime and Punishment,* that his murderer-hero Raskol-nikov rushes into a burning building and saves the life of a little girl. Does that constitute redemption? Or is it not possible—ever un-der any circumstances—for the criminal to *regain* lost self-respect and the respect others once owed him?

These are not outrageous, off-the-wall sorts of questions. They go to the heart of the doctrine of forfeiture, and they raise serious ques-tions about whether or not the doctrine makes any sense. I consider them serious enough to argue that a person *always* has the right to be respected and can never lose that right no matter what he or she does, appears to have done, or is charged with doing. That's why I consider the principle of respect for persons a necessary condition for ethics; it is one of the cornerstones of ethical theory.

ARE RIGHTS ABSOLUTE? One of the very few philosophers to have "bitten the bullet" on the issue of nonforfeiture of rights and to take seriously the inviolability of the person is the twentieth-century American philosopher Eliseo Vivas. In his most interesting book *The Moral Life and the Ethical Life*, Vivas insists that human beings have a status unique among all the things in this world, namely, their status as persons, and their moral personality cannot be lost or cast away. This fact is only acknowledged by "the ethical man," however, who, through suffering, has been made aware of the special status of all persons. Vivas tells us that "there resides in the person an intrinsic worth distinct from the total worth of the values he espouses." He explains this by saying that

> the ethical man respects the other person and treats him in such a way as to avoid violating his dignity, no matter how unworthy morally he may be known to be. For him, beyond moral distinctions lies the intrinsic worth of a man which neither vice nor weakness nor accident can annihilate.[4]

Admittedly, there are problems with the claim that the status of persons is somehow absolute and that no one at all, not even Adolph Hitler, Saddam Hussein, or Charles Manson, ever loses the dignity that must always attach itself to persons. But, then—as we have seen—there are problems with the idea of forfeiture as well. From an ethical perspective the problems with the absolute status of persons appear to be less serious than do those of forfeiture. However, this issue I shall leave the reader to decide. In the meantime, I shall return to several other issues surrounding the concept of personhood that I previously left in the air.

SELF-RESPECT AND USING OTHERS AS A MEANS TO AN END. To begin, I shall examine what it means to *use* other persons and discuss the notion of respect for oneself, which is incorporated into the first principle.

Please recall that we are still attempting to grasp the Kantian notion of persons as ends in themselves. Even though I might disagree with Kant over whether respect for persons can be forfeited, I still unconditionally embrace his concept of persons as worthy of respect. In this regard, one of the best discussions of what Kant might have meant by his odd phrase "using others as a means to another end" has been provided by Onora O'Neill, who singles out coercion as one common way persons use other persons. O'Neill does not claim that the only way persons use one another is by coercion, but she may be right that the phenomenon is more common than we might like to admit.

Briefly stated, coercion involves the denial of another's autonomy, or capacity to make choices, which is the key feature of personhood. If, for example, Fred demands that his wife quit her job and stay home, with no regard for what his wife wants, we have a case of coercion, especially if a threat is involved. Coercion, then, is in direct opposition to consent. As O'Neill puts it,

> Morally significant consent will, I suggest, be consent to the deeper or more fundamental aspects of another's proposals. . . . [T]o treat others as persons we must allow them *the possibility of consent or dissent* from what is proposed . . . *making their consent or dissent possible.*

O'Neill argues that respect for persons goes farther than simply avoiding coercion; it is a positive obligation as well. Kant would doubtless agree with O'Neill when she says, "To treat human beings as persons . . . we must not only not use them, but we must take their particular capacities for autonomy and rationality into account."[5]

Coercion, then, denies not only the personhood (autonomy and rationality) of others, but also our *own* when, for example, we *allow* others to coerce us and otherwise use us for their purposes. When we know others are lying or deceiving us, or manipulating us psychologically or physically, it is wrong not to resist such manipulation. Self-respect involves the insistence upon being respected by others, and it is, according to the view defended here, at least as important as our obligations to others. As Kant would have it, we cannot acknowledge our other obligations unless we first acknowledge our obligation to ourselves as persons.

It might be argued, however, that I have not really tested the principle of mutual respect for persons, and I cannot therefore consider it to be a viable ethical principle. That is true. Think about it for a moment, though: What would it *mean* to reject a principle that is a necessary condition for ethical behavior? That would amount to a rejection of ethics itself, which is absurd. Even the ethics of care theorists, who play down the importance of ethical principles, would have to admit that care implies respect. But suppose we were simply to deny that respect for persons *is* a necessary condition for ethics? This is a very difficult question, so let us proceed slowly.

To say that respect for persons is not a necessary condition for ethics is to say that we could treat one another ethically without mutual respect. But what would that involve? If we can make any sense out of this notion at all, it would seem that it means we would treat one another ethically (i.e., we would avoid harming one another, we would treat another fairly and honorably, etc.) not because we *ought* to do so, but because we *want* to. If we don't happen to want to, then, presumably, we wouldn't. This is very nearly what is involved in the ethics of care theory. Or we could argue that ethical treatment results in the greater good for a greater number of people than does unethical treatment—a variation of my third principle, as we shall see in a moment. But then, why should we care about other people? Many people don't care about others. But as soon as we say this, we realize that in some sense they *should*. And the reason they should care is because all persons are ends in themselves and therefore worthy of respect, at the very least. One of the problems with the ethics of care theory is that it does not provide grounds for the notion that care is a duty: It simply says that some people care about others and that good actions follow from that caring. This is true, but the question here is, What if they don't care? What happens to ethics at that point? Clearly, we are in need of a principle to form the cornerstone of our ethical thinking. And that cornerstone is respect for persons. In a word, denial of respect for persons would make ethical behavior totally arbitrary and whimsical. It would ultimately reduce human interaction to a struggle for power, in all likelihood. Which is to say, it would involve a rejection of ethics once again.

Principle #2: Fairness to Others

I mentioned earlier, you may recall, that the principle of respect for persons, while being a necessary condition of ethical behavior, is not adequate by itself to assure that a given action will have ethical worth. For one thing, it is not clear in a concrete case just what "respect for persons" might involve. Obviously, we ought not to lie and coerce people; we ought not to harm them, either. But we need more than simply the principle of respect for ourselves and others, even if we grant that this includes, following Onora O'Neill, taking "their particular capacities for autonomy and rationality into account." We need a principle of *fairness* that will allow us to more fully acknowledge some of the *positive* obligations we have to one another. Let us see how the second principle adds dimensions to our present discussion, especially when ethical conflict involves more than one or two people.

Recall the dialogue that forms the first chapter of this book. In that dialogue Nina suggests to Rick that students be graded according to where they sit in the classroom. Rick is, understandably, outraged and shouts that "it wouldn't be fair!" He's right, of course, and that's Nina's point. In a sense, however, the rights of the students to be respected as persons have been acknowledged in that the situation has been explained to each of them and they have been given the choice to leave; that is, each of them has the opportunity to stay where they are, leave, or scramble to the front of the class and get an "A." But what the situation conceived by Nina creates is the "right" of each student to be treated unfairly. This is unacceptable. Many of us would insist that the students are not being treated with respect because the situation reduces itself to a battle for front-row seats. Whether or not this is true, it is even clearer, as Rick insists, that the situation is not fair. Thus, I introduce the principle of fairness to supplement the principle of respect for persons in borderline cases in which it is not clear just what rights entail.

We could argue that the principle of fairness is contained, somehow, in the principle of respect for persons, in that we cannot be unfair to someone and *at the same time* have respect for them. To a certain extent this is true. But I stated the second principle in a positive way (treat all persons fairly) rather than negatively (do not treat persons unfairly) in order to draw attention to the positive dimensions of ethics, dimensions that might be ignored if we focus exclusively on the concept of respect for persons—which, as we saw, generates a list of *proscriptions* rather than a list of *prescriptions*, things we should avoid rather than things we should do.

"Fairness" is not an especially difficult concept to accept, and this is another reason to introduce it. It seems to be most helpful when we are dealing with groups of people—it is not clear much of the time what it means to be fair to a particular person in a specific situation, unless we mean simply to repay a debt that we owe—and it is easy to grasp on an intuitive level, even in childhood. For example, if we make the mistake of giving a little girl a smaller piece of cake than her friends, she will cry out, "It isn't fair!!" And she will be right! She is learning about discrimination, which is what happens when our second principle is ignored; and if the other children happen to be boys, she is probably learning about sexual discrimination!

Fairness requires that we treat others as we would have them treat us, that we apply the same standards to and have the same requirements of all persons. It demands not only that we respect one another but also that we treat one another with consideration and sympathy. Fairness requires that in life, as in games, we all play "by the same rules"—both written and unwritten.

Adding the second principle, then, assures us that two necessary conditions are made explicit, both of which help to provide content to what might otherwise be a rather abstract and unsatisfactory command to maximize the sum of human happiness. This is my third principle, and I need to examine it in some detail.

Principle #3: Adopt Rules That Increase the Happiness of the Majority of Those Affected by the Rules

This principle is an adaptation of what is called "rule utilitarianism," which is an attempt by contemporary philosophers to improve upon the act utilitarianism of Jeremy Bentham and John Stuart Mill. As initially put forward by Bentham in the early part of the nineteenth century, utilitarianism tended to direct attention away from motives and actions themselves toward the consequences of actions. Bentham was convinced that the rightness of an action was a function of how many people were made happy by that action. The more people an action made happy, the better it was. By "happy," Bentham meant "pleased," and he was convinced that we could weigh and measure alternative courses of action and choose the one that produced the most pleasure, the one that was, therefore, the right action.

Bentham's protégé, John Stuart Mill, found that this simplistic equation of happiness with pleasure yielded some rather peculiar conclusions—such as the conclusion that an hour at an orgy is better (in a moral sense) than an hour of reading Aristotle's *Metaphysics* because it is more pleasant (present company excepted!). Mill, therefore, rejected the identification of happiness as pleasure, although he retained Bentham's concern with consequences. He accepted the idea that right actions maximize *human* happiness—those things that contribute to making us more "virtuous" in Aristotle's sense of that term as I explained it earlier. (Presumably, human beings would not be as happy at an orgy as they would reading Aristotle, even though they might find it more pleasant. That is, an hour of orgy-going would not contribute to human excellence. In any event, pleasure

DOONESBURY

What the President needs here is a principle or rule. *Source:* © *G. B. Trudeau.*
Reprinted with permission of Universal Press Syndicate. All rights reserved.

was no longer the measure of the rightness of an ethical action for Mill.)

The major improvement the rule utilitarians made to Mill's version of act utilitarianism was to direct attention away from specific actions and their consequences to the rules that govern actions. The need for rules—not to mention a recognition of human rights—is suggested in the Doonesbury cartoon printed here. Act utilitarianism appears in the guise of a "cost/benefit" analysis that leaves too many questions unanswered.

ADOPTING ETHICAL RULES. What is the advantage of focusing attention on the adoption of a rule for an action rather than on the action itself? How is rule utilitarianism an advance over traditional (act) utilitarianism? In either case, we are primarily concerned that the consequences of actions be taken into consideration in determining the ethics of actions. But in Mill's version of utilitarianism, focusing as it does on specific actions, certain puzzling implications strike us as soon as we consider specific cases.

Suppose, for example, Fred lends Alice $50. But instead of paying him back when the money is due, Alice gives the $50 to a charity for cancer research. In Mill's view the charitable act is ethically correct because it makes more people happy than the alternative of repaying the debt. But the rule utilitarian would insist that this is not the right thing to do, since if one were to adopt a rule that this sort of thing should be done as a matter of course, it would produce less happiness than if it weren't done and the debt were repaid. And here I am in agreement with the rule utilitarian. I would say that the act of repaying the debt is the right thing to do because—bringing all three of our principles to bear as this will help us find and apply the appropriate rule in each case—the charitable action (1) ignores the promise Alice made to Fred when she borrowed the money, and therefore violates the principle of respect for him as a person; (2) is not fair because it violates the tacit rules of lending and borrowing; and (3) cannot be viewed as right because if we adopted such a rule it would not maximize the happiness of most of those affected by the rule, which necessitates honesty and the keeping of promises. This last point is supported by the observation that if everyone were to refuse to repay debts and give the money to charity instead then it would no longer be possible for people to borrow money when in need. As a result, the fabric of trust that lending and borrowing rests upon would be shredded—and this has serious implications that go beyond lending and borrowing. Add to this the observation that it is unlikely that Alice's donation will bring about a breakthrough in cancer research and we can see what the conclusion must be.

The genius of Gary Trudeau's cartoon lies in the fact that President Reagan is having difficulty finding a rule or principle that would justify the invasion of Panama. This underscores the inadequacy of simple "cost/benefit," or act utilitarian, analyses. It is difficult, perhaps impossible, to adopt an ethical rule that would ignore the rights of human beings. This difficulty nicely demonstrates the need for the first principle.[6] Furthermore, this difficulty may well have been foreseen by Mill. When he first put forward his particular version of utilitarianism in his book by that name, Mill argued for consequences that maximize human happiness provided that one can "assure himself that in benefitting [the majority] he is not violating the rights—that is, the legitimate and authorized expectations—of any one else."[7]

As a closing aside to this section, it is interesting to see how life imitates art. A CNN poll on the Internet during the 2003 war with Iraq asked viewers, "How many civilian casualties would you accept to get Saddam Hussein out?" The options ranged from "less than 1000" to "less than 100,000." There was no option that indicated "none," but the lowest number had the highest percentage (42%) of respondents. Trudeau must have been amused!

The Application of the Three Principles

The first principle draws attention to the status of persons, who are invariably involved in ethical conflict. The second principle supplements the first and allows us to consider numbers of persons and to resolve some of the conflicts that arise between and among the obligations that persons have to one another. Each of these principles is a necessary condition for ethical action, in that actions cannot be ethical if they violate either of these principles. But a third principle is required to draw attention to consequences of actions and to make possible the weighing of alternatives and the rational determination of which of our options is ethically correct, that is, more likely to increase the happiness of those affected by the rule.

We shall see how these principles work in concrete cases later in the book, and it might be a good idea to look ahead and work through a few of these examples at this time. But before we do that, let us consider in greater detail two theories mentioned earlier that call into question the thesis I am advancing here.

Some Thoughts about Virtue Ethics and the Ethics of Care

You may recall, we started this section with mention of virtue ethics and the ethics of care. Those who put these views forward are reluctant to defend ethical principles, stressing the shifting nature of human experience and the difficulty of applying principles "across the board." Of the two theories, perhaps the one that has had the greatest impact is the "ethics of care" movement, which was spearheaded by a psychologist, Carol Gilligan, who was convinced that talk about principles is a peculiarly male approach to ethics. She advanced the notion that women approach ethics differently and, for all intents and purposes, with greater feeling. Women, she notes in her important book *In a Different Voice*, are more sensitive to the needs of others, and therefore more aware of others, and better able to take "the voice of the other" into account in ethical deliberation. As she put it in a later essay, "women's moral strength . . . is an overriding concern with relationships and responsibilities."[8] Now, whether or not we agree that women think differently from men and ignoring completely the question as to which approach is superior, I would agree that notions such as "care" and "compassion" must have a place at the table of ethical thinking. I shall try to bring this out in the next section when I mention the fact that in our ethical thinking we must be able to imagine ourselves to be the victims of wrongdoing. Clearly, both imagination and intuition enter into ethical thinking, which is not precise and does not yield mathematical certainty. And an uncaring individual can act ethically, but it is not clear that he or she can be considered an ethical person. Still, I think, it is a mistake to abandon ethical principles altogether, since they can play a central role in ethical thinking, as I argued earlier. It is quite conceivable that a person simply does not care about other people and, in this case, ethics goes out the window. Or, in a more likely scenario, a decent person can be caught in a moral dilemma and simply not know what to do. It is not enough simply to be a virtuous person or one who cares about others: At times we find ourselves in moral quandaries, and the only way out is by invoking ethical principles. That is the point of the "Calvin and Hobbes" cartoon at the end of this section. But, let me suggest two further examples.

Example #1. Fred owns a toxic waste company that is responsible for safely burying waste from several chemical plants on the East Coast. Fred takes his responsibilities seriously and he is also close to his family, for whom he provides a good living. Fred's brother-in-law, Arvid, is hired to work for Fred at the request of Fred's wife. Unfortunately, Arvid is not very conscientious and Fred discovers that he has consistently failed to fill out invoices and carefully track the waste after it leaves the factory. In fact, Fred has reason to believe that Arvid is burying the toxic waste illegally. Fred confronts his brother-in-law, who makes light of the whole thing. However, Fred gradually comes to the realization, despite the objections of his wife, that he will have to fire Arvid. Now the ethics of care would stress the importance of caring for the brother-in-law who needs the job to feed his family, and it would stress the close relationship between Fred, his wife, and her brother. But the ethical principles we have explored in this section would demand that out of respect for himself and those he works for and with, out of fairness to those who might be affected by the illegal burial of toxic waste, and to maximize the happiness of those affected by the action itself, Fred ought to fire his relative. The ethics of care runs into difficulty when we have decent people who do care about one another but who find themselves on the horns of ethical dilemmas, because they realize that even persons they don't particularly care about also have rights. Principles do not always provide an answer, but they do provide a framework for ethical thinking.

Example #2. In this case, the ethics of care seems to have a stronger footing. It is a case of reverse discrimination. Fred's company, let us say, has a terrible record of hiring minorities. After Fred fires his brother-in-law, several men apply for the job. The search narrows to two men, one of whom is black. Let us say that the black man has less experience in the trucking industry and has never had to deal with federal agencies. But he has been reliable and is bright, is a responsible family man with two children, and seems able to do the job. His competitor for the job is an unmarried white man, two years his senior, who has worked for a trucking company doing precisely what Fred requires of his drivers. He is highly recommended and seems to be the better qualified for the job. Ethical principles would seem to rule out discrimination of any sort—since it flies in the face of the respect we owe to all persons as ends in themselves.

But those who advocate the ethics of care would probably have us select the black man as the one who has systematically been discriminated against and has the greater need for the job.

What do you think Fred should do? Clearly we can see how ethical problems can become complex and cloudy. Ethical principles seem to show us the way, but sometimes our intuitions and strong feelings run counter to our thoughts about what is right and wrong. Virginia Held may have had it right when she pointed out, "Caring, feeling with others, being sensitive to each other's feelings, all may be better guides to what morality requires in actual contexts than may abstract rules of reason or rational calculation, or at least they may be necessary components of an adequate morality."[9] We certainly should not discount these important considerations if we want to think clearly about ethical problems. One thing that might help is to develop an "ethical perspective" from which we can achieve a sense of distance from the problem and see more clearly, perhaps, what we ought to do in a particular case.

No one said it would be easy! But if Calvin could invoke some ethical principles he could solve this ethical dilemma. Can you help? *Source: © 1989. Universal Press Syndicate. Reprinted with permission. All rights reserved.*

Food for Further Thought

You may or may not accept the principles proposed herein. It is difficult to argue for principles, although the view presented here that ethics has to do with our membership in the wider human community does provide a basis for the principles advanced in this chapter. We need to consider what membership in the human community involves—how are we to get along with other human beings and at the same time become more human? The three principles I have proposed are designed to answer this question, but you should weigh this answer critically. If you were to reject one or more of these principles, would you substitute others? Or would you insist that ethical principles are out of place? Do you think the notion of "care," for example, will suffice? Some of the things I have said about the first principle, at least, are troublesome, to put it mildly. Perhaps the ethics of care view is correct, and principles are simply out of place in ethics.

Can we say that "respect for persons" is a necessary condition for ethics? Does this make any sense? Is it a defensible position? If, for example, a lie is a violation of the respect we should have for one another, what about a lie told to save a person's life? What if, let us say, a good friend were hiding in your basement to escape an angry mob and you were asked a direct question by the mob's leader about your friend's whereabouts. Should you tell the truth? Surely not! Some would argue that you have an obligation to lie in such a case.

In the view presented here, however, this is not so. My position maintains that the mob leader has a right to the truth, even though he plans to harm or possibly kill the man hiding in your basement. There is a painful conflict here, and I shall argue later on that in such cases of "tragic conflict" there is *no* ethically right action: We can only choose the lesser of two evils. This does not mean that, as a matter of fact, you would not lie in this case. It simply means that you could not claim on philosophical grounds *that you had done the right thing to lie*. The lie could not be justified in this case because it is wrong—even though it is the lesser of two evils.

Not everyone would accept this, of course. It may, in fact, be totally wrongheaded. The English philosopher R. M. Hare belittles the notion of what I have called "tragic situations" because he thinks that such situations arise out of a conflict between or among intuitions and that once we reason critically by applying what he calls the method of "universalization" correctly (see note 6) the conflict will be resolved.

But does this really get us around the central issue? That is, when we call an action that can be universalized "right" does this alter the fact that it may simply be the lesser of two evils—which is to say that from another perspective that same action can also be viewed as "wrong"?

And what about the claim that rights cannot be forfeited? Does that seem plausible to you? Suppose, for example, the police capture a man who has confessed to killing seventeen young boys after molesting and torturing them. Doesn't it seem ethically right to demand that the man forfeit his life? Isn't capital punishment justified in this case?

But think about the point made in the text. Is there *nothing* the man can do to redeem himself? Can he do nothing—ever—to make amends? To be sure, his subsequent actions will not bring the boys back to life; but, then, neither will his execution. Can we *justify* capital punishment, in this case or in any other case? Is capital punishment ever right? If so, why? The position taken here is that it is never right. What do you think?

2.2 THE ETHICAL PERSPECTIVE

In the last section I proposed three principles that might comprise the ultimate basis of ethical argument. If we seek to incorporate these principles into our thinking about ethical conflict and ethical choices, we will need to adopt a slightly different perspective than we do in our ordinary thinking. I shall call this the "ethical perspective," in which (in the words of Jeremy Bentham) "everybody counts for one, and none of us for more than one."

Of central importance in ethical thinking is the displacement of the self from a place of special privilege. Ethical thinking is "prescriptive." That is to say, when choices are made in ethics, they are not based on what is right *for me*, they are based on what is right *for anybody*. To take an earlier case, it is not merely right for me to avoid using radar detectors; if our argument is sound, it is right for everybody to avoid using radar detectors. The same is true for the case of infanticide: If our argument is correct then it was wrong for the Spartans or the residents of Achebe's imaginary village to engage in this practice *even though they would not admit it.*

The prescriptive, or normative (from "norms"), element in ethical argument bothers many people. It smacks of intolerance in an age that prides itself on its tolerance and its willingness to allow each person to "do their own thing." But think about it for a moment.

If I make the ethical judgment "Sally really shouldn't have murdered the milkman," and if the reasoning that supports this judgment is sound, then it is true for me, for you, for Sally, and for anybody else, that what Sally did was wrong. The key element here is contained in the little word "if." It allows us to avoid intolerance in ethics: We are all bound by the conclusion *if* (and only if) the reasoning is sound.

We have seen how difficult it is to avoid prejudice in ethics—and elsewhere. We shall soon see how difficult it is to justify our ethical judgments, that is, to support them with facts and sound argumentation. The process of ethical argumentation is fundamentally open-ended. We can never be certain that our judgments are free of prejudice or that the reasoning that supports them is totally sound. *That* is why we must remain tolerant, because we may have made a mistake in our reasoning—not that there is no "correct" answer in ethics (there may be), but because we're never sure we have reached the correct answer! If we can avoid obvious blunders, wrong-headedness, and obvious mistakes we can be reasonably sure we are at least on the right track. That may be the best we can do. But because I reject relativism and the attendant notion that ethical judgments are true for you but not necessarily true for me, I am committed to the view that there is a "right track," and we are all bound by the strength of the argument support for those judgments that seem to place us there. This puts considerable burden on the process of ethical argumentation and necessitates a firm understanding of what makes an ethical argument sound. That will be our objective in the chapters that follow. In this section we need to focus carefully on that perspective that is unique to ethics and that will enable us to think more clearly about ethical matters: the ethical perspective.

Features of the Ethical Perspective

> The ethical perspective involves three aspects: (1) a concern for the consequences of one's actions, (2) neutrality (as far as this is possible), and (3) imagination, which allows us to put ourselves in the place of others who happen to be the victims of ethical wrongdoing.

Except for the third aspect, in which such feelings as outrage, compassion, and sympathy are clearly involved, the ethical perspective requires that we become *distanced* from the ethical conflict in order to eliminate bias or prejudice as much as possible. In the words of R. M. Hare, we must move from the "intuitive level" to the "critical level" of moral reasoning in order to resolve ethical conflict. As Hare notes, "although the relatively simple principles that are used on the intuitive level are necessary for human moral thinking, they are not sufficient."[10] The ethical perspective helps us move to the critical level in our ethical thinking.

This is not to say that "gut feelings" and moral intuitions are out of place in ethics, or that they should be removed in the critical process along with bias, superstition, and fear. It simply means that we must deal with them critically, since even the strongest feelings are not always totally reliable, and some people simply do not have them. To be sure, our gut reaction to such things as cruelty and insensitivity in our fellow human beings can indicate the presence of an ethical problem: Reactions are an excellent starting place for ethical reflection. But we must resist the temptation to rely on those feelings and intuitions without subjecting them to critical scrutiny. It is doubtful, for example, that the torturers at Auschwitz lost any sleep over the cries of their victims or that the gut feelings of the most zealous members of the Inquisition did anything but reassure them that they were doing God's holy work when they burned "sinners" alive because of their aversion to pork.[11]

As I mentioned at the end of the last section, we can all readily admit how much easier it is to think clearly about people who lived in the distant past and with whom we have had no acquaintance. Time and place sometimes afford a natural distance; but it is also possible, if we adopt the ethical perspective, to achieve distance even in the face of immediate personal conflict. Let us examine in some detail how the ethical perspective functions.

Feature #1: Concern for Consequences

As a general rule, most of us are motivated, most of the time, by self-interest. Unfortunately, from the ethical perspective, we are usually motivated by *short-run* self-interest, what we *want* here and now. In ethics it is essential that persons who would do the right thing consider the consequences of their actions, and these consequences may show quite clearly that what is right is not the same thing as what we want to do in this situation—unless we happen to be saints! This means that if we are to act ethically we must attend to the long-run and consider long-run, or "enlightened," self-interest rather than short-run self-interest.

No one on earth knows better than you what you want. You are, therefore, the ultimate authority on what is in your own short-run self-interest. On the other hand, there are things that we all *need*, and these things are not necessarily what we want. When we distinguish between what we want and what we need, we shift attention from short-run to long-run self-interest and we must acknowledge that none of us is necessarily the ultimate authority on matters of long-run self-interest. The consideration of consequences requires thought, imagination, and, at times, the advice of others. To take a simple example, few of us want the dentist to drill a tooth, but we all recognize the fact that at times we need just that.

Short-run self-interest is narrowly focused on the here and now. Since long-run self-interest incorporates a concern for needs, it has a broader focus. As mentioned, it is sometimes referred to as "enlightened" self-interest, and it centers around our membership in the human community, which, as we saw in the last section, is of vital

Background: Mark Slackmeyer is interviewing members of the "Homeless Community" in Lafayette Park at Thanksgiving time, a time described as "the highlight of the homeless social season. . . . Hot turkey, cranberry sauce, the works!" The group is to be entertained by the "Dumpster Divers," and in this panel Mark is interviewing one of the members of that group. As Trudeau points out, it is not always easy to consider the "long term!"

Source: © G. B. Trudeau. Reprinted with permission of Universal Press Syndicate. All rights reserved.

concern in ethics. Indeed, if one were to take the notion of "enlightened" self-interest seriously, one might discover that it involves the same three principles we discussed in the last section: respect for persons, fairness, and the happiness of those affected by our actions. Short-run self-interest, in contrast, has little (if anything) to do with ethics, since it focuses on the individual in isolation from others.

Above all else, the ethical perspective has at its center the idea of what we *ought* to want, what we need as human persons or members of the human community. The moment we begin to reflect on the consequences of our actions, we begin to take others into account. The more we consider the consequences of our actions in the long run the more we realize that our own (true) self-interest is bound up with the interest of others. Our needs are almost always *human* needs, as we saw in the last section. Let us, however, be clear about the other two features of the ethical perspective mentioned at the beginning of this section.

Feature #2: Neutrality

The ethical perspective also incorporates impartiality, or neutrality, as we consider the effects of our actions upon others, all of whom count equally. That is, we should consider the claims of all persons as equally binding and none as any more basic than any others—and this includes our own claims as well. No one counts for any more than anyone else from the ethical perspective—not you, not me, and not even your great Aunt Tilly who will surely leave you a small fortune when she dies![12]

We must consider all persons equally in determining the rightness or wrongness of possible actions, and, as the agent of ethical actions, we must not be biased in our own favor. It is this feature of the ethical perspective, more than any other, that generates a concern for human rights and makes us aware that ethical concerns are global and include all human persons.

But, here again, those who defend the ethics of care will object that neutrality in ethics smacks of indifference. People do care about one another, and well they should. If my child were drowning alongside another child, I would try to save my own child—and that seems to be the "right" thing to do. In situations such as these, principles can't help us, either. We are faced with what I have called a "tragic" situation. But that is no reason to abandon ethical principles altogether and opt for an ethics of care that ignores the question, "What if we do NOT care?" In ethics, one must always be aware that persons, all persons, are "ends in themselves," and worthy of respect. We cannot order someone to care for or love another person (we can, but it will be ineffective); but we can insist that all persons are worthy of respect, regardless of how debased or wicked they seem to be. We have seen how this raises difficulties when it comes to criminal behavior, but the alternative to universal human rights based on respect for all persons is whimsey. And whimsey has no place in ethical thinking. We should care about others, as Carol Gilligan has emphasized, but we cannot be made to care about some people; it doesn't even make any sense to admonish people to care about others. It's a matter of disposition or character: One either cares or she does not. That's simply a question of fact. Therefore, we are forced to fall back on the notion that we should *respect* all persons, whether we like them or not. That was Kant's point, and it is the cornerstone of any workable ethical system. But it is not as easy as it may seem. One thing that can assist us, however, is trying to achieve some sort of distance from our problem. Hopefully this will allow us to achieve a level of neutrality that recognizes the humanity in every person.

But, admittedly, the notion of neutrality is not at all straightforward. The idea is that we shouldn't play favorites in ethics: Everyone counts just as much as everyone else. But, do *you* think it is possible, or even desirable, to remain neutral in ethical quandries?

As you consider this, let us turn to the final feature of the ethical perspective, which, if we are able to adopt it, will assist us in our ethical thinking.

Feature #3: Imagining Oneself as Victim

With the exception of thinkers such as R. M. Hare, philosophers seldom consider the importance of imagination in ethics; but, as Hare insists, it is central. Intuitively, the easiest way to see that an action is wrong in a particular case is to imagine that it is being done to oneself. This, one might suppose, is the point of the so-called Golden Rule, to do unto others as we would have them do to us. For example, I would be less likely to steal if I were to imagine that I am the one stolen from, less likely to cheat and lie if I

Hobbes is helping Calvin imagine himself to be the victim of unethical behavior! *Source:* © *1989. Universal Press Syndicate. Reprinted with permission. All rights reserved.*

imagine myself the one cheated and lied to, and less likely to discriminate if I imagine myself the victim of discrimination. To quote Hare once again, "It is [knowledge of what it is like for the person wronged] which, I am proposing, we should treat as relevant, and as required for the full information which rationality in making moral judgments demands."[13]

The three aspects of the ethical perspective—concern for the consequences of our actions, impartiality, and the ability to imagine oneself the victim of ethical wrongs—combine to help us determine whether a proposed action is right or wrong. We must note, however, that the ethical perspective is nothing more than an aid to intuition. As such this device does not *demonstrate* that a proposed course of action is right or wrong, but it does enable us to place an action in its context and see the implications of that action more clearly than we would otherwise. Furthermore, when used in conjunction with the techniques of critical rationalism that I shall develop in the next chapter, the ethical perspective can be extremely beneficial in helping us to resolve ethical disputes reasonably.

Let us take some examples to see how the ethical perspective works, remembering that what we say is preliminary and in need of further amplification in later chapters.

TWO CASES IN POINT. Let us suppose that I owe you $50 and, since I just got paid today and I know that you need the money to pay some of your bills, it would appear that I am obliged to repay you the money owed. As it happens, however, my wife suggests that it would be fun to go out to dinner and a movie. Since I haven't gone out with her for a while, I decide to accept her offer. Unfortunately, after I have paid my bills and spent the money for dinner and the movie I will not have $50 left to repay you. Should I take my wife out for the evening? If we examine the question from the ethical perspective the answer seems clear: It would be wrong. There really is no argument on the side of taking my wife out for the evening: I simply *want* to do so. This is nothing more than short-run self-interest and does not count from the ethical perspective, from which the obligation to repay the debt is quite strong—as a moment's reflection will attest.

1. The long-run consequences of not repaying the money I owe
   you involve inconvenience and even possible harm to you,

since for all I know you may owe money to others. In addition, even from a narrow, selfish viewpoint I may not be able to borrow money from you, or anyone else, if I don't repay my debts.

2. If I think about it even briefly I would have to admit that if I didn't *want* to have an evening out with my wife (using your money) the issue would never have come up. Thus, I have a decided interest in the matter.

3. Finally, I would certainly not like you to go out for the evening with money you owed *me*.

All three dimensions of the ethical perspective converge to impress upon me the obligation to repay the debt. Thus, what I *ought* to do is repay the debt. But is this what I *would* do?

Let us take one further example to help us clarify the ethical perspective. Consider the following example from a popular British mystery that ran on BBC a few years ago, called *Foyle's War*. In this episode, the year is 1940 and Britain is at war with Germany. Things are not going well for Britain, and Foyle, a middle-age policeman, wants to join the war effort, along with every other able-bodied man and woman. His supervisor turns down his many requests to be transferred on the grounds that he needs Foyle to remain where he is and solve crimes. Indeed, the crime Foyle is working on as the episode begins is a murder. The wife of a prominent citizen, who happens to be German, has been killed while riding horseback in the country. Soon after her murder, the proprietor of a small inn in town is run over by a car and is also dead. Foyle finally solves the crime and the villain turns out to be the murdered woman's future son-in-law who, as it happens, is working for the Navy trying to break Nazi codes that are costing Britain lives. The guilty man confesses to both crimes, and he tries to impale Foyle on the horns of the following dilemma: "You can arrest me, they will try me, and I will almost certainly be hanged, even though the woman was in all likelihood a Nazi spy, sending secret messages to her brother in the German Army back home, and the man I ran over was a known blackmailer and petty crook whose life wasn't worth a tinker's damn. However, my role in the Navy is critical for the war effort. If I am arrested and taken away from my job the advances we have made in breaking the Nazi codes will be set back months and it will cost our country countless lives." Let us say that this is true, that this man's role in the war effort is critical. What should Foyle do? Again, consider what he *should* do as a separate question from the question of what Foyle *would* do.

BEING ETHICAL OFTEN CONTRASTS WITH BEING PRACTICAL. In the "real" world (the world outside the halls of academe?) it may be the case that we rarely do what we should do, unfortunately. But there is a fundamental difference between determining what we *ought* to do and determining what we probably *will* do. This point is related to the rejection of short-run self-interest as an ethical reason. Much of what we do (in fact) is, as I have noted, motivated by what we want to do; ethics, however, requires that we carefully consider those things that we ought to do—whether or not we want to do them. Let us consider the difference between ethical considerations and considerations of short-run self-interest a bit further.

I might note at the outset that separating the ethical issue from the practical issue and matters of self-interest can help greatly in our deliberations about ethical options. It certainly helps to simplify what can be immensely complex issues. We can (and must) always return to the question of how we implement an ethical choice, but at first it will help if we can narrow our focus and attend to the prior question of just what is the right thing to do. *Knowing* what is the right thing to do in a particular case does not guarantee that we will *do* the right thing. But one can be much clearer about what the right thing to do is if one ignores, at least at first, concerns about what one wants or what one regards as in his or her self-interest. If we decide that it would be right to tell the truth in a particular case, as determined from the ethical perspective, we may decide to lie anyway. All I am saying here is that the latter decision needs to be kept separate from the former.

Often situations demand that we "keep our mouth shut," or "toe the line," and it becomes difficult to do the ethical thing even though we know with some certainty what should be done. But this is a *psychological* problem, not a philosophical one. The fact that one has difficulty doing what one has determined to be right has nothing to do with the question of how we determine what the right thing is. It has to do with the need to reconcile ourselves to the fact that at times we must do what we have determined to be wrong.

Thus, even though we must be "realistic" and "practical" and recognize that people do not often (seldom?) do what they should do (what they think is ethically right), we must continue to focus on the ethical reasoning process itself, rather than on the practical problems of actually doing the right thing. Saying that an action is not practical does not mean that it is not right. Philosophy can be enlightening and useful in ethical conflict by helping us to determine what the ethical option happens to be. But philosophy cannot help us to direct our actions in accordance with that option.

I acknowledge that ethical reasoning may well be ineffective because our society, and the workplace in particular, does not place a premium on ethical behavior. But that is no criticism of the *reasoning process* that simply helps us determine in a given case what the right course of action is. Most of us easily follow the course of action that is in our short-run self-interest. Ethics is frequently, if not always, in conflict with short-run self-interest. That is what makes it so hard to do the right thing.

SHORT-RUN SELF-INTEREST AND DUTIES TO ONESELF. To say, however, that short-run self-interest does not count as an ethical reason requires argument. It is certainly not self-evident, and a number of ethical theorists would disagree with this claim. Whatever support we might find for the claim would probably incorporate some of the features of the ethical perspective, described here, such as our claim that ethical reasoning requires neutrality and centers around a concern for others, for the human community, if not the community of all living creatures. A hermit would have few, if any, ethical conflicts: The formation of societies and human communities generally imposes on all who would be members of those communities certain ethical obligations, as we saw in the last section. At the moment we need to stress that the difficulty with short-run self-interest is that it ignores others and focuses on the self in isolation: "You don't really matter; I'm the only one who counts!" The person who thinks this way has not adopted the ethical perspective and is likely to do the right thing only accidentally, if at all.

Those who want to hang on to the notion of short-run self-interest as a legitimate ethical reason would insist that it makes perfectly good sense to talk about "ethical egoism," or the view that we have ethical obligations to do whatever is best for ourselves—not necessarily what we want for ourselves, but what is best for ourselves. The important notion here is the implied claim that we all have duties to ourselves (even the hermit), and it would appear that by ruling out short-run self-interest as a legitimate ethical reason I am ignoring those duties. We are, it might be said, members of the human community ourselves—or most of us are—and we have the same duties to ourselves that we do to anyone else. Thus, if we recognize our duties to others as legitimate ethical reasons, then we should acknowledge the legitimacy of short-run self-interest as well.

My position, on the contrary, is that we can acknowledge our duties to ourselves without bringing in the notion of short-run self-interest. From the ethical perspective we acknowledge that all persons should be regarded as having the same claims. Therefore, to be sure, we have duties to ourselves. But short-run self-interest is not a "duty"; it is something we *want*. Thus, we can count the duties we have to ourselves as legitimate ethical concerns while, at the same time, we ignore short-run self-interest. Further, since we have strong natural inclinations to do what we want to do, we don't need to claim ethical status for what we want to do anyway!

Food for Further Thought

Before reading any further you should carefully consider whether or not you accept the claims I have made thus far. Are you willing, for example, to accept the claim that short-run self-interest does not count as an ethical reason? It does not count, I am saying, because ethics requires that we adopt a neutral stance. From that stance we find compelling only those reasons to undertake a course of action that would persuade anyone *else* that it is the right thing for him or her to do as well. Personal calculations and practical considerations, I am saying, are *irrelevant* to the ethical question because they are simply matters of short-run self-interest. Do you agree with this?

Another question worth considering is the following: Even if we grant that short-run self-interest does not count as an ethical reason, is it *possible* for a person who wants to do the ethically right thing to do so? Or are all motives really motives of short-run self-interest in disguise? If people do everything for reasons of self-interest—a view called "psychological egoism"—then it is not possible for anyone to have "ethical reasons," or reasons that reflect a concern for other persons or are at times in direct conflict with self-interest.

The view of psychological egoism is extremely difficult to refute because even if we find other motives operating in particular situations, the view insists that *real motives* are frequently unconscious, hidden even from the person himself or herself. Thus, if a woman, say, were to decide to tell the truth because she found the reasons to do so persuasive, the psychological egoists would dismiss this entire process as a sham. According to them, all of us simply do what we want to do, nothing more and nothing less. Any attempts to find other reasons for our actions—such reasons as duties to others or to ourselves—are merely various forms of self-deception and subterfuge that allow us to fool ourselves into thinking we are good people when we are simply doing what we want to do. Psychological egoists consider ethical argumentation, as a whole, a form of self-delusion.

What do you think? Can you think of any personal experiences that seem to fly in the face of psychological egoism? What about second- or third-person experiences? Are there no selfless motives? Suppose, for example, a starving mother in Nigeria grabs a crust of bread and, instead of wolfing it down herself, gives it to her child. Is it accurate to say that she acted out of self-interest? Or is it more accurate to say that she was primarily concerned about her child? We might agree that she gets satisfaction from the act, but her satisfaction followed her action and does not appear to have been the motive for it. Or does it? Does this example constitute disproof of psychological egoism? If not, what would refute a theory that makes ethics impossible? What about a young soldier who throws himself on a hand grenade to save his fellow soldiers? Would such an example be a problem for the psychological egoist? Or *is* ethics impossible, a form of self-delusion?

I must consider one final point before I leave this section: The "ethical perspective" as it is presented here totally ignores the question of motive. Do you think motive should be considered a part of any position that professes to provide a perspective on ethical issues? Immanuel Kant, for example, insisted that motive was at the heart of ethics. The classical attack on Kant's view was presented by G. E. Moore early in this century when he insisted that good motives make actions "praiseworthy" but only consequences make them "right." For example, if a physician tries to save a patient's life by administering a drug and in doing so kills the patient, Moore would say that the physician's motive was praiseworthy, but he did not do the right thing. What do you think? If the psychological egoist is right, of course, we cannot have ethical motives: We all act out of self-interest, simply. But if the psychological egoist is wrong and there are ethical motives—obligations to do the right thing—can we talk about an "ethical perspective" without considering motives?

When I presented three ethical principles in the last chapter, I borrowed a principle from Kant that insists upon respecting persons, but I did not agree with him that motive is of central importance in ethics. However, the important question here is: What do *you* think?

NOTES

1. Immanuel Kant, *Lectures on Ethics,* New York: Harper and Row, p. 121.
2. Thomas Aquinas, *Summa Theologica,* 2a–2ac, lxiv 2 and 3.
3. Kant, *Lectures on Ethics,* p. 197.
4. Eliseo Vivas, *The Moral Life and the Ethical Life,* Chicago: University of Chicago Press, 1950, pp. 328–329.
5. Onora O'Neill, "Between Consenting Adults," *Philosophy and Public Affairs,* Vol. 14, no. 3. Italics in the original. Reprinted in Bayles and Henley, *Right Conduct: Theories and Applications,* New York: Random House, 1989, pp. 81–90.
6. One of the most interesting rule utilitarians writing today is the English philosopher R. M. Hare, whose version of utilitarianism arises from his adoption of a Kantian view and centers around what he calls "universalization"—an adaptation of Kant's categorical imperative that turns Kant into a utilitarian of sorts. See, for example, R. M. Hare, *Moral Thinking* (Oxford: Clarendon Press, 1981), p. 50, where he says that a "clear-headed utilitarian and a clear-headed Kantian would find themselves in agreement once they had distinguished between [intuitive and critical] thinking.") Universalization requires that we critically test moral principles by asking what would happen if *everyone* were to act as we propose to act in a given situation. Hare is convinced that his position avoids the shortcomings attributed to many versions of utilitarianism of "riding rough-shod" over reciprocal human rights—which he, too, considers central to ethics. The view I have taken here simply makes the centrality of rights explicit and augments rights with fairness as necessary conditions for ethical behavior. Hare would almost certainly consider this unnecessary since he insists that "the 'right to equal concern and respect' that can be established by appeal to purely formal considerations is nothing but a restatement of the requirement that moral principles be universalizable" (p. 154). What this means is that a principle that is in violation of human rights (and fairness?) could not be universalized—we cannot imagine that anyone would be prepared to act on a principle that would entail willing harm to himself/herself.

Be that as it may, the version of rule utilitarianism defended here involves Aristotle's doctrine of human happiness as the desirable end of ethical actions (rather than Hare's "interests of the people in society considered impartially"). As such it is more straightforward, and the notion that rights and fairness comprise necessary conditions to ethical actions seems easier to adopt for critical purposes—especially for beginning philosophy students. Hare's book might make excellent supplementary reading, however.

7. J. S. Mill, *Utilitarianism, On Liberty, Essay On Bentham*, New York: Meridian Books, 1965, p. 270.

8. Carol Gilligan, "Why Should a Woman Be More Like a Man?" in *The Pleasures of Psychology*, eds. D. Goleman and D. Heller, New York: New American Library, 1986, p. 41. Please note that by stressing "respect for persons" here I emphasize the fact that human rights are derivative. That is, my claim to be accorded my rights is a function of my respecting your rights as a person. I think that this formulation avoids the bifurcation that Gilligan, for one, finds in the masculine/feminine approach to morality—women favoring responsibilities and relationships, men favoring rights and rules. In my formulation rules are secondary and must yield to respect for persons and fairness as necessary conditions for morality (see Gilligan, *In a Different Voice*, Cambridge, Mass.: Harvard University Press, 1982, p. 19).

9. Virginia Held, "Feminist Transformations of Moral Theory," *Philosophy and Phenomenological Research*, Vol. 50, 1990, p. 332. The student who is interested in the history of ethics might note that the ethics of care has strong similarities to the "moral sense" theories of, especially, the Scottish philosophers in the eighteenth century. As Terry Eagleton has noted in this regard, for the moral sense theorists, "before we have begun to reason, there is already that faculty within us which makes us feel the sufferings of others as keenly as a wound, spurs us to luxuriate in another's joy with no sense of self-advantage, stirs us to detest cruelty and oppression like a hideous wound" (Eagleton, *The Ideology of the Aesthetic*, Malden, Mass.: Blackwell Publishers, Inc., 1998, p. 39). As Eagleton notes, the subjectivity of this view, like that of the ethics of care, makes it difficult to treat it as a systematic ethical theory.

10. R. M. Hare, *Moral Thinking*, p. 39.

11. In an age that tends to idolize feelings, it is reassuring to find a psychologist who sees the need to subject feelings to critical scrutiny. James Hillman makes the following comment in this regard: "The terrorist and the girl who kills for her cult-hero (Charles Manson) also trust their feelings. Feeling can become possessed and blind as much as any other human function. . . . Feelings are not a faultless compass to steer by; to believe so is to make Gods of them, and then only Good Gods, forgetting that feeling can be as instrumental to destructive action and mistaken ideologies as any other psychological function" (Hillman, *Re-Visioning Psychology*, New York: Harper and Row, 1975, p. 182).

12. In his important book *A Theory of Justice*, John Rawls was apparently intent on incorporating this notion of impartiality into his argument. He proposed the notion of "the original position of equality," which requires that each of us consider questions of fairness and justice through a "veil of ignorance." Behind this veil we lack any particular knowledge about any of the individuals who are involved in the ethical conflict we are addressing; we cannot pursue our own short-run self-interest because we don't know what that is! Behind the veil of ignorance I do not know whether I am rich or poor, black or white, male or female, victim or victor. The notion stresses the fundamental ethical equality of all human beings in the original position. As Rawls put it, "with this adjustment no one is able to formulate principles especially designed to advance his own cause. Whatever his temporal position, each is forced to choose for everybody" (Rawls, *A Theory of Justice*, Cambridge, Mass.: Harvard University Press, 1971, p.140).

13. Hare, *Moral Thinking*, p. 92.

Interlude

Rick and Nina Revisited

RICK: I've been thinking about our talk the other day and there are a couple of things that continue to bug me.

NINA: Oh? Like what, for instance?

RICK: Well, like the fact that people who think there's some kind of absolute right and wrong tend to be dogmatic and intolerant. I'm not saying *you* are, but people who take your point of view frequently are. If there's one thing we've learned from history it's that people who think they've got the "truth" about how other people should live their lives tend to go around shoving their ideas of right and wrong down everyone else's throat!

NINA: I don't blame you. That sort of thing has always bothered me, too. But what people do when they think they've "got the truth" (as you put it) doesn't affect the question of whether they do or do not know something you and I might not know. After all we don't know everything!

RICK: Neither do they. That's what bugs me.

NINA: They might not know everything, but they could still know something you and I don't know. We've got to be careful that we don't confuse two separate issues, though.

RICK: What two issues?

NINA: First, whether it makes sense to say that people can know if there is a right and wrong when it comes to human actions, and, second, why they behave as they often do when they think they *do* know.

RICK: OK. Let's agree that these are two separate issues. How do we deal with them?

NINA: Well, I'd ignore the second issue. I'm not qualified to say why people tend to become intolerant when they think they know something someone else doesn't know, especially when it comes to right and wrong. But, I do think it makes perfectly good sense to say that people *can* reason about right and wrong and that they can reach reasonable conclusions. That may not be "knowledge" and it certainly isn't "absolute," but it isn't ignorance, either.

RICK: Oh, so you admit we can't know about these things?

NINA: What I think is that infanticide (to take our previous example) is *either* right *or* wrong: It cannot be both, regardless of where and when it is practiced. If the stronger argument suggests that it is wrong (as it seems to me it does) then I think it reasonable to conclude that it *is* wrong unless or until we can come up with new arguments one way or the other. It's as though there may be an absolute right and wrong, but we can't know it absolutely!

RICK: If we can't say for sure what it is, then why bother about it at all? Why not just talk about what people *think* is right or wrong?

NINA: I have no problem with that; no one can say that he or she knows with any certainty what is right or what is wrong. But you must admit that what some people think is sometimes more reasonable than what other people think. And a great many people don't even bother to think about ethical issues at all. They simply insist it is all a matter of feeling. But, it seems to me the more reasonable position is more likely to be the "correct" position in some sense. At any rate, we can certainly think about it and talk about it as you and I are doing. But this needn't lead to dogmatism and intolerance, since the process is left open to new arguments and new evidence.

RICK: That's another thing that bugs me.

NINA: What?

RICK: Your preoccupation with what is "reasonable." Why do you make such a big deal out of this anyway? Why should we prefer reasonable positions to unreasonable ones? Sometimes it's a good thing to cut loose and do what everyone else calls "unreasonable." What about feelings? You just seem to toss them out in a heap! How can you exclude feelings from ethics, anyway? You, of all people!

NINA: I don't exclude feelings. I don't see how anyone could think about something like infanticide and *not* have strong feelings about it! I'm just not sure what to say about them. For me they're a good place to start, but I'm not sure we can rely on feelings altogether: I don't think we can say infanticide is wrong just because I have strong feelings of antipathy toward it.

RICK: Why not?

NINA: Because I might just as easily *not* have those strong feelings, or, worse yet, I could have strong feelings in *favor* of infanticide! And yet it still seems to me reasonable to insist that killing innocent babies is ethically wrong regardless of our feelings.

RICK: There you go again! Who's to say it's reasonable? To me it is perfectly reasonable to say that infanticide is right for those who are used to it and do not feel antipathy and wrong for those who do.

NINA: Then there's no real disagreement? Just different feelings?

RICK: Exactly!

NINA: And, I gather, if a person doesn't feel anything one way or the other, infanticide is neither right nor wrong?

RICK: Sure. Why not?

NINA: But what about those of us who try to provide some basis for our claims, some sort of evidence and argument, over and above any feelings we might have?

RICK: So what? People like you *feel* that an argument is required, so you muster one up.

NINA: So there's no such thing as a weak or a strong argument, just arguments and the way we feel about them?

RICK: Well, I'm not so sure in general. But in ethics it may be so.

NINA: What do you say about the fact that occasionally (at least) an argument or evidence can change the way we think or feel about something, even in ethics? What do you say about the fact that you can have strong feelings that something is wrong and yet an argument can persuade you that it's right despite your conflicting feelings?

RICK: What do you have in mind?

NINA: Well, homosexuality for example. I know you're practically homophobic on the topic: you have strong feelings of disgust about homosexuality and yet you cannot provide any arguments to support that view. I might even be able to present you with a strong argument to convince you that homosexuality is not immoral or unethical and you might have to agree regardless of how *you feel* about it.

RICK: So?

NINA: So . . . the argument is not simply something we attach willy-nilly to feelings; arguments and feelings can function independently of one another, but the way we think about things can change the way we feel about them. There can be strong arguments in support of positions we feel deeply are wrong. And if the argument is strong, that is, we cannot find any way to weaken it, we must accept its conclusion regardless of how we feel. We might even find our feelings on the topic start to change! But we have little or no control over such things. We must focus our attention on the strength or weakness of arguments that do or do not support ethical claims. If there is a strong argument in support of a practice such as homosexuality, and if someone still feels that it's wrong, but can't show why, then he or she is probably mistaken. Moving the issue to the level of argument and evidence and removing it from the level of personal feelings allows us to consider ethical conflict as an arena of genuine agreement and disagreement and requires that we continue to search for reasonable positions and abandon unreasonable ones regardless of how we feel. It allows us to resolve ethical conflict reasonably. That's pretty important, it seems to me.

RICK: Well perhaps so. It all sounds like a lot of trouble. But I still worry about your idea of what's "reasonable." We could take any six people at random and get six different definitions of what that word means. In addition, I doubt whether any one of them would recognize it if they saw it!

NINA: You're probably right about that, at least as far as "reasonableness" is concerned. But they would have less trouble recognizing what is "unreasonable"! That's why we look for and reject unreasonable positions in ethics. Incoherence, inconsistency, contradiction, and downright factual inaccuracy are pretty easy to spot. We can even spot unreasonable prejudices. After we have rejected a claim as "unreasonable" we can suppose that the claims that are left, which we have no grounds to reject, are reasonable.

Further, if I can support an ethical claim with an argument that is strong, it seems reasonable to say the claim is probably true. But that's hardly dogmatic or intolerant. The process is always open to correction and modification and we're never sure we have reached "the truth." The only thing we insist upon is that there *is* a "truth," and we seek to apprehend it *by degrees* through the process of critical thinking.

CHAPTER THREE

Devising a Procedure

3.1 CRITICAL THINKING SKILLS

I have stressed the fact that relative claims differ from nonrelative claims because of the type of support (or lack of support) the different claims have. What this means is that when ethical conflicts arise, attention should shift from the claims themselves ("Brutus shouldn't have killed Caesar") to the support for those claims. That support can be in the form of other claims (Brutus miscalculated Caesar's ambition; furthermore, the Republic became an Empire under Caesar's nephew Octavian despite Caesar's death), or in the way the claims go together to make an argument.

I should mention at the outset of our discussion of arguments that there is something called the "burden of proof," which is placed on the person who wants to make a case for a view that is unusual or out of the ordinary in some way. Not everyone need take upon himself or herself "the burden of proof," but only the one who wants to make a claim that is *not generally accepted*. Suppose, for example, that I want to insist that the earth is flat. The burden of proof is on me to show this because it is generally agreed (by this time) that this is not true. In ethics, the burden of proof is on the one, for example, who insists that Sally was completely justified in killing the milkman for leaving whole milk instead of skim. This is not generally accepted; therefore, the "burden of proof" is on the one who makes such an "outrageous" claim. What this means, then, is that if you are taking a position that is generally accepted, you do not have the "burden of proof." You may be able to put together a very convincing and strong argument for your position. But you do not need to do so. If you are challenged, your opponent is obliged to assume

81

the burden of proof. The reason it works this way is that what is generally accepted, on the grounds of common sense, is probably true. It may *not* be true, of course, but if it is not, the "burden of proof" is on the one who thinks it is not. In a court of law, of course, the jury is directed to presume the defendant innocent until proven guilty. The burden of proof in our legal system is always on the prosecution.

There are three things that can occur in connection with the burden of proof. To begin with, a person can simply accept the burden of proof and try to make the best possible case for the position that is not generally accepted in order to persuade people to change their minds. This is what Copernicus did in trying to make a case for the heliocentric hypothesis. Second, one can simply ignore the fact that the burden of proof is on his or her shoulders and simply insist that something is true even though no one else agrees. When this happens, the informal fallacy of "appeal to ignorance" is frequently committed. We will cover a number of informal fallacies in the next section, but it might pay to take a quick look at this particular fallacy.

Suppose I insist that ghosts exist. This is not generally accepted, so the burden of proof is on me. But I may ignore this and simply insist that ghosts exist because "no one has ever proved that they do not exist." This is a crude attempt to avoid acceptance of the burden of proof, to avoid making any sort of real argument, and it is a very weak position to take. A claim is not true simply because it hasn't been proved to be false, nor is it false because it hasn't been proved to be true. To argue in this way is to commit the fallacy of "appeal to ignorance."

Finally, one can try to "shift" the burden of proof to the other person—even though that person is maintaining a position that is widely viewed as correct. Generally speaking, the attempt to "shift" the burden of proof from your own shoulders to your opponent's, even though his or her position is the commonly accepted one, is a bit sneaky and underhanded because the generally accepted position is assumed to be true until or unless it can be shown to be false, and it thus doesn't require argumentation.

One of the most notorious examples of shifting the burden of proof came in the confrontation between Galileo and the Roman Catholic Church over the Copernican theory discussed in the previous chapter. The Church's position was that the Copernican theory could pass as a hypothesis, unlikely (and even silly) but harmless in the face of the Ptolemaic theory that was widely accepted and fit well into accepted Church doctrine. That is, the burden of proof was on those who would displace the Ptolemaic theory with the new, Copernican theory. In what had to be one of the most outrageous moves in history, Galileo wrote a letter to the Jesuit Bellarmine in which he insisted that if the Church's position conflicted with the "demonstrated truth" of Copernican theory, then the Church had to prove the Copernican theory wrong! This attempt to *shift* the burden of proof was one of the main reasons the Church finally brought Galileo before the Inquisition and forced him to recant.

To review, if one is adopting a position that is uncommon or in any way out of the ordinary, that person should accept the burden of proof to show why it is the correct position and the widely accepted view is somehow wrong. This is, of course, difficult to do. But it is not impossible. Second, one can simply ignore the responsibility of the burden of proof and insist that he or she is correct because the view he or she defends has never been shown to be wrong. This tactic commits the informal fallacy of "appeal to ignorance." And finally, one can try to shift the burden of proof back on to the shoulders of the one who is objecting to the unusual or uncommon claims and try to make them prove their point—even though it really doesn't require argument. In a way, if you think about it, committing the fallacy of appeal to ignorance is a way of shifting the burden of proof to the other person. ("I know I am on weak grounds here, but no one has yet proved my claim to be false. Thus someone else must prove it to be false or I will continue to believe it to be true.") But it certainly is fallacious—as we shall see in the next section.

Keep in mind in reading this chapter that, as mentioned at the outset of this book, the word "argument" does not mean what it means when your cousin Dudley and his buddy Al argue over whether the Lakers will take the NBA championship again this year. That is, it does not involve shouting and throwing half-empty beer cans at one another, although if Dudley and Al ever calm down they might offer reasons *why* the Lakers will (or will not) take the NBA championship this year. In this book, supporting a conclusion with reasons that can withstand criticism constitutes an "argument."

In fact, even if it doesn't comprise a "good" argument, it is still an argument, as the word simply refers to a *form* of presentation that involves premises (claims presumed to be true) and a conclusion (presumed to be true because the premises are true). Even if the argument is not a "good" argument, that is, if it commits some sort of fallacy or cannot withstand criticism, it may still be an argument. That is to say, even though an argument is not very strong, or "good," it may still be an argument, in the sense that something is asserted as true (the conclusion) because other claims (the premises) are considered to be true. What I would like to put forward in this book, however, are "good" ethical arguments, that is, arguments that *can* withstand criticism and seem to be strong. That is my goal.

The Argument Structure

It is important that we learn how to construct and deconstruct arguments and what it is that makes them good (strong) or bad (weak). An argument always has a point to make, called the "conclusion." In thinking about an argument the first thing we must do is determine (a) whether or not it *is* an argument and, if it is, (b) what the conclusion is. All of the steps in the argument link together in a chain or web to support the conclusion. These steps are called "premises" or, simply, "reasons." There are two types of arguments, inductive and deductive. Most of the arguments we deal with on a daily basis are inductive, that is, the conclusion is not necessarily true even if the premises are. In a deductive argument (which is rare) if the premises are true and the argument follows certain formal rules—which are taught in a logic course—then the conclusion *must* be true. This is called "strict implication," or "entailment," and in the case of deduction, a valid argument, that is, one that obeys all the rules, states a conclusion that is *necessarily* implied by the premises. Most of the time, because we are dealing with inductive arguments, the relationship between the premises and the conclusion is much looser, and even if the premises are true the conclusion is, at best, merely "probable." In either case, the conclusion usually is identified by an *indicator term*, such as "therefore," or "thus." We also frequently use indicator terms that suggest reasons rather than conclusions, indicators such as "because" or "since." The most common indicator terms are the following:

Conclusions	Reasons
therefore	because
thus	since
it follows that	as
consequently	for
hence	in view of the fact that
which means that	given that
so	inasmuch as

Unfortunately, when arguments are put forward, sometimes there are no indicators at all, making our job more complicated. In addition, indicators such as "since" may not be logical connectors at all because "since" can also refer to *time,* as in "I've been here since 3:00 P.M. yesterday afternoon." We must decide when we see the indicators whether or not there is a logical connection (as there was in the previous sentence when I used the word "because") and *even if we do not see any indicators* we must still determine whether there is a logical connection. In other words, if we suspect that an argument might be present, we must look for logical connections between the statements: If we find indicators, fine; if not, we must decide whether the connections are there anyway, hidden away or merely unstated. The easiest way to do this is to insert a reliable indicator where we think one belongs (such as "therefore" or "because") and see whether or not it changes the meaning of the passage in which we suspect there might be an argument. Let us take a couple of easy examples to clarify this important point. Note that the names are fictitious, to protect the innocent!

Example #1

The Supersonics look solid again this year because Johnson is back, along with Peterson; the team signed their top three picks from last year's draft; and they also signed Mayberry, who was a free agent. They have been there before and they know how to play under pressure. None of the other teams has really done much to improve. The Lakers are getting old, Janson finally retired in Washington, and they didn't get anyone to replace him. I just don't see anyone else coming out of the woodwork to win the NBA championship.

Analysis

This is an argument containing the reliable indicator "because" that points to the latter portions of this passage as the reasons or support for the (implied) conclusion, which is that "the Supersonics will take the NBA again this year" (implied by the phrase "look solid again"). We haven't asked whether or not this is a strong or "good" argument yet; we must determine first whether it is an argument at all. It is. And it happens to be an inductive argument because there is no necessity whatever between the premises and the conclusions, only probability. Note that the word "because" could have been left out and it still would be an argument. That is, if we had said that "the Supersonics look solid again this year. Johnson is back, . . . " we could insert the indicator "because" and we could see the logical connection that exists between the first statement (the conclusion) and the rest of the passage (the reasons). The important thing to note is that there *is* a logical connection between the reasons and the conclusion, as there is in any argument, inductive or deductive. Take another passage where there is no such connection.

Example #2

The Celtics will take the NBA championship again this year. Your cousin Dudley is a big Celtics fan, the Timberwolves got a new mascot this season who looks like Rin Tin Tin, and the Lakers cheerleaders are getting new costumes.

Analysis

There are no indicators here. Furthermore, if we put one between the two sentences we change things considerably, imposing a different meaning on the passage. There simply is *no logical connection* between these statements. This passage is an example of what is called "exposition," and it differs from argument in that the statements are disconnected and there is no point, or conclusion, to the passage.

The "WHY?" Question

If we are not sure whether there is an argument in a given passage, one reliable test is to ask "the why? question." If statements are connected together logically, asking "Why?" after any given statement that *seems* to be the conclusion will help us determine whether or not it is, in fact. Arguments are *directional*: They lead from premises to conclusions. Asking "Why?" after what seems to be the conclusion will direct us back toward reasons when they are present. Take another example, again, another inductive argument.

Example #3

The Vikings are riddled with dissension and have no team unity. The Bears are at least a year away as yet, and the Lions are the only other team in the division to pose any threat. But they don't match up well with the Packers. The Packers will dominate the Division again this year.

Analysis

As you read this, you might suspect that the final statement is the conclusion. All the statements appear to be connected, and they seem to lead toward that final statement. Put that claim first, and then ask "Why?" and see what happens:

"The Packers will dominate the Division again this year." WHY? "Because the Vikings are riddled . . . (etc.)." We have an argument, it has a conclusion, and there are reasons that support the conclusion. The fact that the reasons, or premises, do not *necessarily* imply the conclusion (that is, it might be false even if the reasons are true) indicates that we are dealing with an inductive argument. (Remember: Deduction can yield necessity, induction can only yield probability.) Insertion of the indicator "because" doesn't change the meaning of this passage; it simply makes it clear that an argument is present. Contrast this with Example #2 and note how asking the "Why?" question in the earlier example would not have directed your mind toward either the first or the second statement. That is because the statements have no logical connection with one another. There is no "direction" there.

Suppressed Premises

As if things were not complicated enough, we quite often encounter arguments with suppressed or missing premises. As critical thinkers we must discover what those missing premises are and place them in the argument where they belong. Although the person advancing the argument has primary responsibility for making it as strong as possible, it is also our responsibility–in accordance with what is sometimes called "the principle of charity"–to give the argument the benefit of every doubt. This sometimes means helping to complete an incomplete argument.

A deductive argument is like a chain, and the weak link is often found in the missing premise, or unstated assumption, that is supposed to hold the argument together. It is important, therefore, that we know how to find these assumptions and make them explicit so that we can examine the argument and determine whether we should accept the position it advances.

When an argument fails to include a step or a reason, that is, when an assumption is being made, we need to ask ourselves what *else* must we know, besides what is given, to allow us to grant that particular conclusion. That "something else" is frequently the assumption. Take another example.

Example #4

Rudy can't possibly be a levelheaded person under stress. He's a redhead.

Analysis

There is an argument here, believe it or not! When we ask the "Why? question," it leads us to the first statement as the conclusion and the second as a reason. We can then insert an indicator term, as follows:

> "Rudy can't possibly be a levelheaded person under stress because he's a redhead."

Clearly, however, there is something missing. Ask yourself: What *else* must I know to grant the conclusion? The answer can be found by looking for a term that appears in the conclusion but nowhere else in the argument. The assumption will have something to do with that term. As a rule, in any argument if a term appears in the conclusion but nowhere else in the argument, an assumption has been made. In this case, the missing premise will have something to do with being levelheaded under stress, since that term suddenly appears in the conclusion and nowhere in the premises. We need to find out what is assumed to be generally true about this quality. The answer is the claim that "redheads are not levelheaded persons under stress." Now as it happens this is a very weak claim, and it is a very weak link in this argument as well. We can set it up as follows:

> "Rudy can't possibly be a levelheaded person under stress because he's a redhead, and redheads are not levelheaded persons under stress."

In the next section we shall see why this is a weak argument.

Remember: Look for indicators. They will help you find the conclusion if there is one. Ask the "Why? question" if you suspect there is a conclusion, and try inserting indicators where you think they should be. If you think you have located the conclusion, insert a reliable indicator (such as "because" following a conclusion or "therefore" preceding a conclusion) and see whether the passage has retained its meaning or changed somehow. If you simply do not see any connection between any of the statements and no one statement seems to stand out as the conclusion of the passage, you probably are not dealing with an argument. Your common sense is a fairly reliable guide, but careful reading is essential.

Evaluating Arguments

If you are dealing with an argument and you have located the conclusion (and any missing premises) you are halfway there! The next step is to determine whether or not the argument is strong.

The strength of the argument is determined by asking two fundamental questions:

1. Is the support (reasons, or premises) factually correct or at least plausible?

2. How close is the connection between the reasons, or premises, and the conclusion?

Let us take the first item. For testing the plausibility of reasons, the most reliable method is that of "counterexamples." If, for example, I insist that affirmative action programs invariably lead to hiring quotas and are therefore discriminatory, you might counter with examples of such programs that have not led to discrimination in the past. Such counterexamples will weaken my claim that is supposed to support my conclusion and thus weaken the argument as a whole. The more counterexamples we can provide, the less plausible the claim becomes and, therefore, the weaker the argument.

We can also counter support claims (premises) by simply refuting those claims that purport to be factual. If one were to insist that blacks are inferior to whites—as many did in the nineteenth century—because they are less intelligent as a result of a smaller cranial capacity, we could counter by showing that "inferiority" is not a function of intelligence, that there is no logical connection between cranial capacity and intelligence, and/or that blacks do not (in fact) have a smaller cranial capacity than whites.

We should note that even when we cannot verify the truth of a claim given as a reason in support of an argument, strictly speaking, we can still tell whether or not it is a "good" reason, that is, whether or not it is *plausible* in the context of the argument. This process is called "weighing reasons" (sometimes "winnowing reasons") to determine whether or not they support the conclusion. The same process is employed in ethical decision-making to determine which of two or three choices seems to be the right thing to do. The trick is to question those reasons that require further support, or those reasons that are incoherent or inconsistent with what we generally accept as true (they just "don't fit"), and to look for those that remain after the critical process has been completed. This is the Socratic *maieutic.* Two things are important in this process: (1) Keep a critical attitude (while remaining open-minded), and (2) ask good questions!

Connecting Premises with Conclusions

The techniques for scrutinizing the connection between premises and conclusions are a bit more complicated than simply adopting a critical attitude and asking good questions, unfortunately. It goes back to the difference between deductive and inductive arguments explained in the previous section. What we need to do is to determine whether there is a "gap" between the reasons given and the conclusion that purportedly rests on those reasons. In a strong argument the premises are true (or plausible) and there is little, if any, gap between premises and the conclusion. The absence of a gap between premises and conclusions signals a deductive argument whose conclusion is necessary if the premises are true and the rules of formal logic are all followed, as I said earlier. If there is a gap between premises and the conclusion, then the conclusion is merely probable and we know we are dealing with an inductive argument. The wider the gap the lower the probability, until it gets so wide there is no connection between premises and conclusion at all!

The word "gap" is a metaphor suggesting that in the case of low probability it is possible to reject the conclusion even if we accept the premises—we might even draw *another* conclusion. As I mentioned earlier, arguments are directional: They lead us from the reasons to the conclusion. If there is a gap between the reasons and the conclusion, we can change directions and go to another conclusion. Where there is no gap we have a case of strict logical necessity: If we accept the premises as true, and the rules of formal logic are all followed, that is, the argument form is a valid one, we *must* accept the conclusion as stated whether we want to or not!

Argument Chains: Strict Entailment

As noted earlier, in deductive arguments that exhibit strict necessity, or what logicians call "entailment," premises are linked together in such a way that the conclusion becomes another link in what is an intellectual chain, but one that is only as strong as the weakest link. What this means is that if any one of the premises can be shown to be false, the entire chain is weakened and the conclusion does not follow—even if the rules of formal logic are obeyed. We say, in such a case, that the argument is *unsound*. If the weak link, or premise, cannot be strengthened by further argument support or new factual evidence, the argument as a whole fails. We can see this by means of a simple example:

Example #5

1. Socrates was a man.
2. All men are mortal.
3. Therefore, Socrates was mortal.

This is a classical case of strict entailment in a deductive argument. The premises (sentences 1 and 2) are linked together (by means of the common term "man") to support the conclusion (3). If we grant that the premises are true, the conclusion necessarily follows, and we have no choice but to accept it. Even if we don't know the formal rules of logic, we can tell that this is a valid deductive argument because we can sense that *if* we accept the premises as true, we would *have to* accept the conclusion as true also (whether we want to or not). Inductive arguments do not yield this sort of certainty. However, even in this case, if one of the premises were false—let us say historians prove that Socrates never lived—the entire argument would break down. If we can break one link (premise) in the chain, the entire chain (argument) is destroyed.

Argument Webs: Probability

As it happens, most of the conclusions we try to reach are not *strictly* implied by premises we can say are true; they are more or less plausible as the premises are more or less likely to be true. That is, when we are dealing with *inductive* arguments, there is almost always some gap between premises and conclusions. Such arguments can *still* be strong, however (though never "valid"). Arguments involving probability between reasons and the conclusion are strong if their premises are true (or plausible) and the gap is narrow between those premises and the conclusion they support. In such cases the conclusion is likely to be true, even though it is not logically necessary. We would say it is "highly probable." Generally, the wider the gap between premises and conclusions, the weaker the argument; the narrower the gap, the greater the probability and the stronger the argument.

The point has been well put by David Kelly in his excellent logic book, *The Art of Reasoning*. Kelly tells us that

> we assess strength by seeing how much free play there is between premises and conclusion. The technique is to assume that the premises are true, and then ask whether there could still be a reasonable doubt as to whether the conclusion is true. Assuming that the premises are true, is the stated conclusion *the only one consistent with the evidence they provide*? In that case the argument is strong. Or are there other conclusions that would be equally consistent with the evidence? In that case the argument is weaker.[1]

To recall the analogy used earlier, the premises of an argument involving strict, logical necessity are linked together to form a chain: We might say that the premises of an argument that involves probability form the strands of a spider web (as Kelly would have it). The more strands of the web there are, the stronger the argument becomes—even though we will not find strict necessity here. We can weaken the argument by attacking and breaking down one strand, or premise, but we do not thereby destroy the argument as a whole. Let us take another example:

Example #6

(1) Harry is hard of hearing, and (2) has poor vision. He (3) has had three speeding tickets in the past two months, (4) several minor accidents and (5) one major accident in the same time period. I say, then, that (6) Harry is a poor driver.

Notice the lack of common terms in the premises, which have no logical connection with one another. Rather, they are simply a series of separate and independent considerations that converge on a conclusion that is supported by the premises, but not strictly implied by them. The conclusion, indicated by the term "then," is likely to be true if the premises are true, but we could accept all of the premises and the conclusion might *still* be false (Harry might have attended driving school since these incidents—or, perhaps he stopped drinking!). Furthermore, we could show any premise to be false (Harry has 20/20 vision, let us say) and yet the argument is still fairly strong. The argument does not fall apart the way the chain argument in Example #4 does. There are plenty of *other* reasons why Harry should lose his license!

If you think back to the example in the last section, about the short-tempered redheads, you can see why it is a weak argument. The assumption ("All red-heads have short tempers") is clearly false. Thus even though it obeys the rules of logic (it is valid), it is not sound. To be "sound" a deductive argument must be *both* valid and have true premises. This is the strongest possible type of argument. But it is rare.

Consider Both Entailment and Plausibility

Whether or not we find ourselves dealing with premises that are connected like links in a chain or like strands in a spider web, the argument strength depends upon the truth or plausibility of those premises and the way the premises are connected to the conclusion. In the rare cases when conclusions are strictly implied by their premises, the argument collapses if one premise is shown to be false, as in the case of short-tempered red-heads. In the more common, inductive, arguments in which conclusions are more loosely connected to their premises, the argument is weakened, but not destroyed, if a premise is shown to be false.

We should note that implication is a purely *formal* relationship between premises (reasons) and conclusions. By itself it cannot dictate that an argument is strong because arguments can still be weak even though the conclusion is strictly implied by the premises, again, as in the case of the red-heads. As I have said, the strength of an argument is a function of *both* necessity (or probability in the case of inductive arguments) and the truth of the premises: If the premises are not true—or even if one premise is not true—the argument is weakened. On the other hand, even if the premises are true, if there is a gap between the premises and the conclusion (if there is no necessity or low probability) the argument is also weak. Consider Examples #7 and #8 in this regard.

Example #7

All short men are insecure, and since Fred is a short man, he must be insecure.

As in the case of Example #4 (the red-heads again) the conclusion of this argument is strictly implied by the premises indicated by the words "and since." If we accept the premises, we *must* accept the conclusion, which is necessary, given the truth of the premises. However, we do not have to accept the premises as true. Surely, the first premise, "All short men are insecure," is false, just as the assumption in example #4 was false; it comprises the weak link in this chain and destroys the argument. Not only must the conclusion be supported by the premises, but the premises stated must also be true, or at least plausible.

Another example will illustrate the contrary condition. With true premises but no necessary implication the argument also fails.

Example #8

Harry has poor hearing and weak eyes. Further, he has received several speeding tickets in the past couple of months, during which time he has also had several traffic accidents. Therefore, Harry is a rotten husband.

The premises may be true, but the conclusion does not follow from those premises. There is no connection here whatever (note the lack of "direction")—just a large gap between the premises and the conclusion. Indeed, we should draw a totally different conclusion, the signal that we are dealing with a very weak argument. The reasonable conclusion to draw from these premises is that Harry is a poor driver—not that he is a rotten husband!

> The paradigm case of a strong argument, then, is a deductive argument in which the conclusion is strictly implied by the premises given and those premises are true, or very likely to be true. If the argument is inductive, the implication is not necessary, it is merely probable. But there can be some very strong inductive arguments—even in ethics!

Illustrations

Let us take some more examples, working from weaker arguments to stronger arguments in order to see how to determine which are which.

Example #9

REPORTER: Senator, would you please explain why you voted for the experimental bomber, especially in light of the cost overruns and the widespread criticism of that particular plane?

SENATOR: Certainly. I will be glad to. It is imperative that we have a safe and secure defense system, that we keep America strong and our enemies weak. The surest way to squander our precious heritage is to knuckle under to our enemies abroad, and peace can only be guaranteed by a strong defense.

Analysis

If we say that the senator's conclusion is that America's defenses must be strong and we assume along with him that the experimental bomber is necessary to maintain that strength (which is doubtful), there is still little, if any, connection between the reasons he gives and the conclusion he wants to draw. That is, even if we accepted the reasons the senator gives, we might still refuse to accept the conclusion as true—there is a gap between the reasons and the conclusion! Indeed, a different conclusion altogether might be said to follow from those same premises. Consider, for example, whether or not we would be "knuckling under" to our "enemies" by cutting back on our defense spending. Why should we accept this as true? It is certainly not self-evident, and the senator gives no support for this claim. An important issue being ignored here is whether or not our present defenses can adequately deter the "enemy" and ensure peace. Peace may not require continued military spending. But even if it does, it is not clear why the experimental plane must be part of that spending. There are several problems here, and *the argument's tendency to wither under scrutiny suggests that it is rather weak.* A stronger argument would not invite as many questions and doubts about its premises, and it would have a tighter connection between the premises and its conclusion. In fact, as we shall see, this argument commits an informal fallacy! Take another example.

Example #10

The fact that a majority of the States, reflecting after all the majority sentiment in those States, have had restrictions on abortions for at least a century seems to me as strong an indication as there is that the asserted right to an abortion is not "so rooted in the traditions and conscience of our people as to be ranked fundamental." (*Roe v. Wade,* J. Rehnquist, dissenting)

Analysis

This is an inductive argument, and it is fairly strong, certainly stronger than the previous one. If we accept the premises we are likely to accept the conclusion that is supported by those premises and is unstated but obvious from the position Rehnquist takes on this issue. If we stated it, we might put it this way: "Therefore, I do not consider abortion a fundamental human right." But the first statement is questionable: Why accept the claim that *because* states "have had restrictions on abortions for at least a century" *therefore* the sentiment in those states is in opposition to abortion? What sort of restrictions do those states have? How can we be sure that the laws in those states reflect majority sentiment? How old are the laws restricting abortions in those states? Even though they might have reflected majority sentiment at one time, can we say they still do? We can see that there are a number of important questions that must be answered before we can grant the truth of the premises, and asking pertinent questions is probably the best way to scrutinize an argument. Thus, even though there is very little gap between the reasons stated and the conclusion we imagined to follow from those reasons, the conclusion must remain in doubt until we can establish stronger plausibility for the reasons—either by way of further evidence or argument. An even stronger argument follows.

Example #11

Certain chemicals are known to cause cancer in laboratory animals, and when this happens there is a likelihood that these same chemicals will cause cancer in humans. It would seem prudent, therefore, to avoid these chemicals whenever possible.

Analysis

This is a strong inductive argument. The conclusion is implied by the premises given and the premises appear to be true, although there is a missing premise to the effect that it is prudent to avoid chemicals that cause cancer. Presumably, the author of this argument thought this was self-evident. Note here that the plausibility of the premises is increased by use of such terms and phrases as "there is a likelihood" and "it would seem prudent." When claims are modified by such qualifiers they are stronger than if they are asserted universally by means of such terms as "always" or "never," "all" or "none." We can apply this to the example of hotheaded redheads. It is easier to support the claim that "some" or perhaps even "many" redheads have hot tempers than it is to support the claim that they *all* do! This is a good thing to remember when you consider arguments and when you try to put your own arguments together: You strengthen your arguments by making your claims more modest and you weaken them by making broad, sweeping claims that are hard to support. In fact, a sweeping claim based on slim evidence commits the informal fallacy called "hasty generalization." You will learn about more such fallacies in the next section, but for now be warned that a generalization based on skimpy evidence is fallacious. If your folks are reading the paper and come across a story about college students rioting in downtown Memphis, they might say, "Those college students are always getting in trouble." That would be a fallacy. The story is about *some* college students, not about *all* students. Chances are, many more students were in their rooms studying their ethics!

In Sum: We have seen what a strong argument is and how strong arguments differ from weak ones. We have also learned to "weigh" reasons when we cannot determine with confidence that they are true or false: Those reasons are "good reasons" that are more resistant to criticism; those reasons that cannot withstand critical scrutiny are bad reasons or no reasons at all. The purpose of criticism in the process of ethical reasoning is, therefore, a positive one: to formulate the best arguments we can to support the ethical positions we take and to recognize the more reasonable of several options when we are faced with difficult choices.

3.2 TRAPS AND PITFALLS: INFORMAL FALLACIES

Many of the mistakes in reasoning that all of us make daily are referred to as "informal fallacies," in contrast to violations of the formal rules of logic, which are formal fallacies. Arguments that commit informal fallacies are weak because they result in a lack of implication (a gap) between the premises and the conclusion. The weakness in an argument caused by an informal fallacy is internal to the argument and has nothing to do with whether the conclusion is true or false: It is simply not true or false *for the reasons given.*

We have looked at a couple of fallacies already, hasty generalization and appeal to ignorance. In addition, there are over one hundred informal fallacies that were carefully labeled and discussed during the medieval period by the Schoolmen. But we shall look at only a few of the most common ones that arise in ethical reasoning, fallacies that comprise traps and pitfalls to good ethical arguments.

Ad Populum: Appeal to the People

Almost certainly the most common fallacy in ethical reasoning is the commonplace appeal to "people." When the question of wrongdoing arises, one frequently hears the remark: "What's wrong with that? Everyone does it!" In fact, during the Watergate scandal one frequently heard that what President Nixon did couldn't be wrong because "all politicians do that sort of thing." Now, there are at least two problems with this remark. To begin with, how can we know what "everyone" does or does not do? We can't. But, furthermore, even if it were true it would be irrelevant. Even if everyone (or all politicians) lied to save face, for example, it would not necessarily make it the right thing to do. (You can probably remember your Mom saying to you when you were young, "Well, if everyone jumped off a cliff would you follow?" That's a typical Mom remark, and you should listen to your Mom. She's right about this: Even if it were true that everyone else does something, that doesn't mean it is something you should do.) The question of justification, as we shall see in the next chapter, is much more complicated than this.

As mentioned in the last section, a good critical thinker should become suspicious of any claim that contains the words "every," or "everyone," or "all" and any claim that involves sweeping general-izations or superlatives. Claims such as "Michael Jordan was the best basketball player ever to play the game" simply cannot be proven true or false. Similarly, the claim that "Everyone does it" cannot be proven true or false. We strengthen the claim by making it more modest: "Many people do it," or "Jordan was one of the best play-ers to play the game." Avoid sweeping claims in your own arguments and be wary of them when you see them in others' arguments!

As it happens in this case, even if the claim about "everyone" is modified to make it seem more plausible, it may still involve this fallacy. To be more specific, if I make the seemingly safer claim, "(Almost) every politician plays dirty tricks on the opposition. There-fore, this politician is justified in doing so," I have still committed this fallacy because an appeal to what all or even many others do is a weak appeal in itself—all or most people may simply be wrong! It requires further elaboration.

Put in this bare-bones fashion, can be clearly seen: the gaps in the reasoning that mark this as a weak argument. Everyone (or almost everyone) does X, therefore you ought to do X. It needs to be shown that what "everyone" or "almost everyone" does is right before I can conclude that it is the right thing for you to do. There is a gap here that needs to be filled by further argument. There may be good rea-sons why almost every politician does these things, and there may not. It remains to be shown. This argument's weakness is also evi-dent from the fact that the conclusion stated is only one of several that could be drawn from the reason given, even if we grant that that reason is true.

Straw Man Fallacy

This fallacy occurs in response to another argument. Remember that: It is always in response to another person's argument or general position they have adopted. That's a clue as to how you can identify it. It is an attempt to dismiss the prior argument by making it appear weaker than it really is, to reduce it to a "straw man," so it can be blown away. In fact, it frequently involves a conscious distortion of the previous argument in order to dismiss it easily.

Consider the following exchange that occurred on television a number of years ago. A caller on a phone-in show was objecting that beer and wine commercials should be banned from TV and radio because these ads get young people to drink who might not otherwise do so. The response was that "you can't force people to stop drinking: They've been doing it since the dawn of time." Now, that's a straw man because the caller's position was not that people should stop drinking, but that ads should be removed from TV and radio so as not to encourage young people to start drinking. What the response does is to distort purposely the caller's argument to make it seem silly. There's also a hint of what is called "a red herring" in this response, as we shall see in a moment. This is an attempt to draw attention away from the real issue. Sometimes weak arguments commit more than one fallacy at a time! Keep an eye open for that possibility.

When Nina argues with Rick in our opening dialogue that certain things that happen in other cultures are simply wrong because they violate certain basic ethical principles, Rick would be committing the fallacy of straw man if he were to reply, "You just think everything in our culture is superior to what goes on elsewhere. That's ethnocentrism, and I don't want to have anything to do with that." Notice that this is not what Nina said: It is a blatant distortion of what she said. Nina is not advocating ethnocentrism; she is advocating critical thinking about specific practices across cultures, including her own. This is definitely not "ethnocentrism." The key to the "straw man," then, is that it is a response to a particular argument that distorts that argument in order to more easily dismiss it as weak or somehow wrong-headed.

What may be a classic example of "straw man" happened in a book entitled *The Child-Centered School* written in 1928 that fostered an attack on "traditional" education, which was characterized as the "old school" and likened to a "listening regime," a place of "fears, restraints, and long, weary hours of suppression."[2] There is little ev-idence that traditional education was this awful, but it helps the critic make the case for "progressive" education, since no one in his or her right mind would want to have anything to do with "tradi-tional education" as thus described! Again, the straw man consists in the fact that the opposing position is described in the weakest form possible so that it can be swept away by the critic who is con-vinced that she has a better alternative in mind.

Begging the Question Fallacy

We often hear people say, "This begs the question of whether there should be welfare at all," or something to that effect. What the speaker means is that this "raises the question." The phrase is mis-used. Begging the question is an informal logical fallacy that occurs when one presupposes the conclusion (the question) in the prem-ise, thereby "begging the question."

If I say "school is a waste of time because the time could be bet-ter used," I have really begged the question because the premise "the time could be better used" says the same thing as the conclusion "school is a waste of time." In other words, I haven't really provided an argument at all; I have simply stated the same thing in different words. That's a clear case of begging the question. The premise is supposed to be a reason for the conclusion, not just another way of saying the same thing! The following example, from an ethics book by J. L. Mackie written in 1983, is a bit more subtle: "The death penalty offends moral sentiments or feelings, because the pre-arranged killing of someone at a stated time is a special outrage against human feelings which are an essential part of morality."[3] Boiled down to its essentials, this says "the death penalty offends moral sentiments because it offends moral sentiments." Note the circularity here, which is a sign of begging the question. And also notice how carefully you must read to detect this fallacy! One more example should help solidify this explanation.

Consider the following argument: A favorable response to higher taxes always results in providing better education, since a favorable response to higher taxes always results in better classroom buildings, and better classrooms guarantee a better quality of education.

The question has been begged here. What this person needs to do is to show that better classrooms lead to better education, otherwise she has simply said that higher taxes lead to better education because higher taxes lead to better schools. I said at the outset of this chapter that arguments lead in a direction from premises to conclusion. One senses this direction, whether there are indicators or not. In the case of this fallacy the direction is a circle: It doesn't go anywhere. That's why it is called "begging the question," or "circular reasoning."

One more wrinkle to this fallacy is what we refer to as "question-begging epithets," words that slant an argument in such a way that what we are trying to prove is already affirmed in the premise. If a lawyer says to the jury, glowering at the defendant, "This criminal has shown by his demeanor in this courtroom that he is guilty of the crime as accused," he has used a question-begging epithet—by calling the accused a "criminal"—the very thing he has to show! If you hear, for example, that "no right-thinking American could possibly oppose this war," you should detect the question-begging epithet in the case of "right-thinking American," since the question in this case is what "right-thinking" Americans think about the war (one suspects in this case that "right-thinking Americans" are ones who agree with the speaker!). In the abortion issue, which is hotly contested, a speaker might argue that "babies ought to be allowed to come to full term and not murdered before they even take their first breath"; we can see the question-begging epithets in the use of both "baby" and "murder," since the issue is precisely over whether or not the fetus is a "baby"; if it is not, then it cannot be "murdered." The question (whether or not the fetus is a person) has been begged simply by loading the language of the "argument." As a general rule, it is a good idea to avoid loaded terminology—that is, words heavy with strong emotional overtones—when putting together your own arguments and to keep a sharp eye open to spot them when others use them. The use of scare-quotes around the word "argument" above merely points to the fact that this fallacy removes the claims being made from the realm of argument altogether: It doesn't go anywhere, and no conclusion is established by the support of good reasons. Strictly speaking, this is the case with all informal fallacies.

Illicit Appeal to Authority Fallacy

As a rule, there is nothing "illicit" about an appeal to authority. Indeed, if we could not appeal to authority to establish many of our truth claims, we would be able to make very few claims at all. But some of these appeals are legitimate while others are not. Thus, if my physics book tells me that the temperature on Mars is extremely cold at night, I can claim to "know" that fact on good authority. If, on the other hand, Edgar Rice Burroughs makes the same claim, and I insist it is true because Burroughs says it is true, the "knowledge" is bogus: The claim itself is suspect. The key here is the legitimacy of the appeal to authority. Claims are more or less probable depending on whether or not the authority we appeal to is a legitimate authority on the question at issue or whether there is concensus among experts on the question at issue. If the experts disagree, the appeal is suspect. An "illicit appeal" is an appeal to an authority who happens to be outside of his or her realm of expertise or an appeal to an expert who is in the minority on a particular issue. When it comes to writing science fiction, for example, Burroughs has some legitimacy as an authority. If we wanted to establish the conclusion that science fiction writing is more demanding on the author than writing ordinary fiction because Burroughs says so, the argument contains some plausibility because Burroughs has written both science fiction and ordinary fiction.

Strictly speaking, however, any appeal to authority raises some suspicion: Nothing is true simply because someone or other says so. But clearly some appeals are more legitimate than others. To avoid the fallacy of illicit appeal to authority, one must consider the credentials of the authority appealed to in support of a conclusion,

The presidential candidate interviewed here commits what may be the ultimate appeal to authority! Even though the credentials of the authority are unimpeachable, the claim itself is suspect! *Source: G. B. Trudeau. Reprinted with permission of Universal Press Syndicate. All rights reserved.*

as well as the question of the reliability of the claim made by that authority.

One good rule of thumb in areas in which we feel out of our element (because the questions are too technical or we have no basis for establishing or rejecting credentials) is to ask whether the authority appealed to has any particular ax to grind: An authority that has an ax to grind is less reliable than one who does not. A spokesperson for Exxon who says that an oil spill does not endanger the wildlife of the area is less likely to be a reliable authority than a biologist at the University of Alaska who has no particular job interest in the truth or falsity of his claims!

Appeal to Emotion Fallacy

If I argue that Steve Jones cannot possibly be a murderer because he has such an innocent face, I commit the fallacy of appeal to emotion—pity in this case. There is no logical connection whatever between having an innocent face and having an inclination to murder. As we saw earlier, we could accept the premise (Jones has an innocent face) and draw any number of possible conclusions: (1) His parents must be good looking people; (2) he must have broken a lot of hearts as a young man; (3) he is guilty as sin—no one can be that innocent. But if in a court of law a clever defense counselor points to his client's face with its innocent expression we might very well, as members of the jury, find ourselves moved by that expression to draw the conclusion that the defendant is not guilty—despite the evidence to the contrary. We can also be moved by fear, patriotism, sex appeal, or even love.

Unfortunately, J.J. commits the fallacy of "appeal to emotion" in this exchange.

Source: G. B. Trudeau. Reprinted with permission of Universal Press Syndicate. All rights reserved.

We should be wary of conclusions claimed simply because of assorted appeals to emotions that have no logical bearing whatever on those conclusions. Whether or not we feel strongly about something is not sufficient grounds for claiming that it is right or wrong. It may be a clue, and one worth following up, but by themselves, feelings sway us to unreasonable conclusions much of the time. Having an innocent face (whatever that means) has nothing whatever to do with the question of guilt or innocence in a murder trial.

Red Herring Fallacy

In the "red herring" fallacy, which we came across in discussing the straw man fallacy earlier, a case is made for one conclusion and presented as though it were a case for another, sometimes unrelated, conclusion. Consider, for example, the Doonesbury cartoon on this page.

In this cartoon, Mark Slackmeyer, a disc jockey for NPR, is recounting the names of Reagan appointees "charged with legal or ethical misconduct." The cartoon is the sixth in a series of cartoons dealing with what Trudeau calls "Sleaze on Parade," and Larry Speakes has called Mark to counter his charges.

Speakes refers to the reading of the 103 names as a "vicious smear campaign by the liberal press." Now, whether or not we know what to call this allegation, we can quickly see that there is a flaw in Speakes' logic. Let us put his argument together to see how and where this flaw arises. In doing this we must do a little imaginative reconstructing, since a cartoon does not allow for a full-fledged argument—even supposing that readers demanded such things!

Source: © *G. B. Trudeau. Reprinted with permission of Universal Press Syndicate.*

Speakes' argument appears to be as follows:

(R) Sleaze on Parade is a vicious smear campaign by the liberal press.

(C) Therefore, we should not condemn the 103 appointees, who must be presumed "innocent" persons of "integrity."

An assumption is operating here, of course. It appears to be that (A) such smear campaigns by the "liberal press" slander innocent persons. What is important for us to consider is that the central issue is the guilt or innocence of the 103 appointees whose names are being read over the radio. The flaw in the logic of Speakes' counterargument is that it ignores that issue altogether and diverts attention to another, unrelated issue, namely, the reliability of the "liberal press." The red herring results from the fact that the premise stated introduces an issue irrelevant to the main concern of whether those persons are guilty of "legal and ethical misconduct" while in office. More importantly, and this is where the term "red herring" arises, the irrelevant issue purposely diverts attention from the central issue. The press may or may not be "liberal," and it may or may not slander innocent persons. But the 103 persons whose names are read on the air may still be guilty as charged. That issue has not been addressed.

The same sort of fallacy is committed when someone like the senator in the last section argues for continued development of the experimental bomber on the grounds that opposition to such development is opposition to "a strong national defense." When this phrase is introduced into the debate, attention shifts from the issue of the bomber to the unrelated issue of a strong national defense. It isn't clear, for example, that a strong national defense cannot be achieved by means other than continued development of the experimental bomber. One could accept the reasons given (that we should have a strong national defense) without accepting the conclusion that we should continue to develop the experimental bomber. Once again, a gap exists between the premises and the conclusion: A number of possible conclusions can be drawn from the reasons given, even if we allow that the reasons are all true. This tells us that we are dealing with a weak argument: There is no connection here. Indeed, there is a fallacy, a red herring!

Bifurcation Fallacy (False Dichotomy)

In order to fully understand this fallacy, we need to discuss the notion of contradiction and the related concept of inconsistency. To contra-dict (say against) is to say two things that are mutually incompatible; they cannot both be true—as when I say that my friend is both friendly and mean. Contradiction applies only to the things we say, or the claims we make. For example, one cannot claim that something is and is not the same thing at the same time and in the same respect. My friend may be friendly to some and mean to others, but she cannot be both friendly and mean at the same time and in the same respect. This is logically impossible. All contradictions are inconsistent, but inconsistency is a broader notion than contradiction and applies to actions as well as claims. If I claim to be a proponent of "the right to life" but am in favor of capital punishment, then I am being inconsistent. If I say that a fetus has a right to life but a convicted criminal does not, my claims are inconsistent and, perhaps, contradictory. We would need to make sure we know what I intend to claim in this case. The burden of proof would be on me to show how the two cases differ. On the face of the claims themselves, there appears to be a contradiction. And, most assuredly, we need to avoid inconsistency and contradiction in our ethical arguments. These are cardinal sins of critical thinking!

Bifurcation occurs when we take a statement that either "a" is true or "b" is true and simply assume that they cannot both be true or ignore entirely the possibility that "c" or "d" may be true. In such a case, we say that the disjunction between "a" and "b" is exclusive (both claims cannot be true because it would involve a contradiction) when, in fact, the disjunction may be inclusive (both claims may be true, in fact, or some third claim might be true—there is no contradiction). Inclusive disjunctions can both be true, as when I say "I am going to lunch. I haven't made up my mind yet, but I probably will have either soup or a sandwich." I could have both, neither, or some third dish I discover upon entering the cafeteria line. Most disjunctions take the form of either/or, and they are inclusive. The classic case of bifurcation arose during the Vietnam conflict and has reared its ugly head again in our "War on Terrorism." It takes the form of "America: Love it or leave it." This is bifurcation. One can love America, criticize it, and remain a loyal citizen. One doesn't have to love blindly or move else-where. Furthermore, one could both love her country and leave it. There would be no contradiction here. As is always the case in bifurcation, this form of reasoning is a type of oversimplification that tends to reduce disjunctions to exclusive either/or statements without allowing for the possibility that there are other options. (See the cartoon on this page.)

In a more serious vein, consider the following brief, typical ar-gument over abortion:

> If you are in favor of abortion you are in favor of infanticide: you're either "pro-choice" or "pro-life"—there is no middle ground on this issue. Now I've heard you say many times that you're in favor of abortion. Therefore, you're advocating infanticide: You're in favor of the killing of innocent babies.

This is an example of oversimplification in the form of bifurca-tion, coupled with reliance upon a very vague catch term, "pro-life." It is not at all clear that everyone who opposes abortion is "pro-life." Nor is it clear that everyone who is "pro-choice" is not "pro-life." For example, one could be against abortion but in favor of war and the death penalty, or opposed to war and the death penalty but in favor of abortion in certain instances, although, as we saw earlier, there is more than a hint of inconsistency here. The term "pro-life" is a misnomer in these cases. Additionally, many who ap-prove of abortion on demand deny that the fetus is an infant and would object to the term "infanticide" and consider it a form of begging the question, in this case insisting that the fetus is an in-fant and that abortion is therefore murder.

Unfortunately, J.J. commits the fallacy of bifurcation. *Source: © G. B. Trudeau.*
Reprinted with permission of Universal Press Syndicate. All rights reserved.

The bifurcation appears clearly in the phrase "you're either 'pro-choice' or 'pro-life'—there is no middle ground on this issue." Ruling out the middle ground, or third or fourth alternatives, reduces the disjunction "either/or" to exclusive terms and does not allow for shades of gray. In the "real world," as they say, shades of gray abound and we must beware the tendency to disallow this middle ground—which may be the reasonable ground to take. Be on the watch for constructions of the "either a or b" type. They may involve bifurcation.

In sum, beware of inconsistency and contradiction in what we say and do. And beware of simplification in our thinking, as when we claim either that one is a loyal citizen or that one criticizes the decisions of those in power—forgetting that there is no contradiction in saying that one can do and be both at once. Most of the time, unless we are stating a contradiction, things can be both one thing and another, both loyal and critical, blue and black, red and orange, sweet and sour, tall and short (tall in one respect, short in another). The key is whether or not we would be stating a contradiction if we claimed both were true at the same time and in the same respect. If there is no contradiction involved, chances are the disjunction is inclusive and we can have it both ways!

Ad Hominem: To the Person

The *ad hominem* ("to the person") fallacy is committed when we try to direct attention away from another person's argument to something we find objectionable about the person himself or herself. There are several types of *ad hominem* fallacies (circumstantial, *tu quoque*, etc.) and you would be well advised to take a course in logic and learn all of them. But for our purposes, just as we did in the case of the appeal to emotion, we will focus our attention on the main problem: The fallacy is committed because the person is attacked and not the argument. The tactic can be very effective, of course, because—like all of the fallacies—it makes a strong appeal to our feelings rather than to reason. If we are not careful, we will find ourselves convinced that because Jones is conservative (or liberal) what he says cannot make any sense. This is nonsense, of course, and we must evaluate the strength of Jones' argument on its own merit, regardless of which way he leans politically. But, make no mistake about it, this is a very common error as we find it easier to label the person than to consider his argument carefully and thoughtfully. It can go so far as to "poison the wells," as one version of the *ad hominem* is called, where we refuse to consider a person's arguments at all, since we have determined ahead of time that he or she can't possibly be correct because that person is a _____ (fill in the blank).

As a tactic, it can be used quite effectively in a court of law; a prosecutor, for example, might try to persuade the jury that the witness' testimony cannot be reliable because, let us say, the witness is a prostitute, a drug addict, or a felon. Now there is an element of truth here, as there is in many fallacies, and this is why we must be so careful. If a person is a known felon then it is quite possible that his testimony will not be reliable. But, on the other hand, we cannot infer that *because* the witness is a known felon, *therefore* his testimony is false. This simply does not follow. In the case of eyewitness testimony where there is no other corroborating evidence, we might have better grounds for rejecting the felon's testimony, but we are not on solid logical ground when we do so. If at all possible, one would try to find other evidence to support or refute the testimony of a witness known to be, generally, unreliable. But, again, we cannot infer anything at all about what a person says from the fact that a person is of questionable character. Just because Fred is a card-carrying member of the Communist Party does not allow us to infer that what he says is therefore bogus. Like it or not, we must listen to what Fred has to say and evaluate his argument on its merits.

False Cause Fallacy (Post Hoc, Ergo Propter Hoc)

If you remember nothing else from what you have read in this book, try to remember the wonderful Latin phrase "*post hoc, ergo propter hoc*," or simply "*post hoc.*" If you toss it about, your friends will be impressed and your parents convinced that their money is well spent on your education! The phrase means "after this therefore because of this," and it is the label for a rather common fallacy. We commit this fallacy when we insist, for example, that because one event follows another event the latter must be the cause of the former.

Now, establishing causal relationships is extremely difficult, as any scientist will tell you. One of the reasons the tobacco companies were able for years to defeat attempts at lawsuits was because of the fact that no one could prove that smoking causes cancer. In order to prove that A causes B, for example, one must show that whenever we have A we also have B and we cannot have B without A. That is, if A is a cause of B then it is the necessary and sufficient condition for B. There are smokers who never get cancer and there are people with lung cancer who never smoked, so the question of whether or not smoking causes cancer was for many years in question. To insist that it was would be to commit the *post hoc* fallacy, and that is what the tobacco companies relied upon. What was eventually established was an extremely high correlation between smoking and lung cancer, and this correlation, coupled with the fact that the tobacco companies knew of it and continued to deny it (as revealed in inter-office memos), while making a concerted effort to get young people to start smoking, eventually made it possible to win in court against Big Tobacco.

To take one more contemporary example, let us consider the controversy over what has been called the "self-esteem movement" in the public schools. This movement has been around for nearly fifty years and dominates educational philosophy in the grades. Simply put, advocates of this view insist that we can raise Suzie's and Fred's academic performance simply by telling them, again and again, that they are wonderful, or, as one author recently put it, "telling them they are good for no good reason." Advocates argue against such things as competition and grading and insist that teachers should befriend their students and that if students fail it is the teacher's fault. There are a number of offshoots of this movement, including the so-called P-C movement and the push for multiculturalism in its many guises. One such guise is the Afrocentric movement, whose advocates range from the rather militant to the subdued. In one experiment with the Afrocentric movement in Washington, DC, in the mid-1990s, Superintendent Franklin Smith worked closely with Albena Walker to establish a school-within-a-school involving approximately 150 students who focused heavily on African subject matter. The school was called the "Webb School"; after six months, when compared with a comparable school, "the Walker curriculum led to more parental involvement, better self-esteem among students, higher test scores on the Comprehensive Tests of Basic Skills, and less disruptive behavior in the classroom."[4]

Now, self-esteem advocates might jump on this test case to show that higher test scores resulted from the improvement in self-esteem among these predominantly black students. But that would be a *post hoc* fallacy, since the higher scores might also be the result of increased parental involvement, which has been shown to improve student performance. In order to show that improved self-esteem results in higher test scores, another experiment would have to be conducted that, perhaps, eliminated parental involvement. In fact, I know of no such test, and most of the tests that have been conducted over the years to show a causal relation between higher self-esteem and better performance in school have failed to show any correlation whatever—which has not, however, deterred the educational establishment from its commitment to the view![5]

The *post hoc* fallacy is common and we tend to find it convincing until we pause and reflect for a moment. If a Democrat happens to be president at the moment and the economy starts to suffer, we find ourselves tempted to reason that the economy is failing because there is a Democratic president. But, strictly speaking, this is no more reasonable than to argue that because people on a remote island sacrifice virgins to the volcano god and the volcano remains silent, therefore the sacrifice causes the god pleasure and keeps the volcano quiet! Clearly, this is nonsense. But then all of the conclusions that are said to follow from reasons that have no logical connection with the conclusion, that is, all informal fallacies, easily lead to nonsense. That is why we must carefully guard against falling into their emotional trap: They persuade for no good reason.

We need to guard against the use of fallacious reasoning ourselves and to be wary of it when used by others as well. Fallacies, informal though they are, break down the connection between reasons, or premises, and conclusions.

A Word about Analogies

Frequently, speakers and writers will draw analogies between situations they want to explain or defend and more familiar situations. The assumption is that because something is true of the familiar it is also true of the unfamiliar. These analogies, or parallels, are often persuasive and at times rightly so. But they can also mislead and should be considered carefully. If I say, for example, that a nation is like a ship at sea and ought to have only one captain, I am attempting to defend the rule of one person. One needs to realize that there are always dissimilarities between the items being compared and you will need to focus attention on them. The nation is not a ship at sea, even though it may (or may not) resemble it in important respects. If the analogy begins to seem weaker and weaker the more you think about it, it is probably a weak analogy. A strong analogy, one that stands up to close examination, may be very persuasive and allowed to stand. But, in the end, all analogies will eventually break down and they don't prove anything. But they can be persuasive and a powerful rhetorical tool. A good writer uses them carefully, and a good critical thinker is wary.

In order to test your skill at finding weakness in arguments generally, and in finding informal fallacies as well, work your way through the following exercises. Keep an eye open for analogies as well and discuss them with your classmates to see if they are truly persuasive.

EXERCISES

I. Looking for Arguments

In the following exercise, you are asked to read each example carefully and try to determine whether or not an argument is taking place. If it is, circle the indicator term and underline the conclusion. If possible, point out any unstated assumptions and point out the principles involved in cases of ethical argument. Also, watch for unstated conclusions! Remember: There may be an argument even if you find no indicators. If you think there is a logical connection between premises and conclusion, insert an indicator and see if it makes clear that there is an argument taking place. Be alert for arguments within arguments, or arguments whose conclusion is used as a premise for a further argument. You are not being asked to judge the quality of the argument, that is, whether it is strong or weak, but merely to determine whether or not one (or more) is taking place.

1. Socialism is a system based on belief in human goodness, so it never works. Capitalism is a system based on the belief in human selfishness; given checks and balances, it is nearly always a smashing success.

2. The flight from interpretation seems particularly a feature of modern painting. Abstract painting is the attempt to have,

in the ordinary sense, no content. Since there is no content, there can be no interpretation.

3. Since marriage constitutes slavery for women, it is clear that the women's movement must concentrate on attacking that institution. Freedom for women cannot be won without the abolition of marriage. Attack on such issues as employment discrimination, for example, is superfluous; as long as women are working for nothing at home we cannot expect their demands for equal pay outside the home to be taken seriously.

4. There is a perennial classical question that asks which part of the motorcycle, which grain of sand in the pile, is the Buddha. Obviously, to ask that question is to look in the wrong direction, for the Buddha is everywhere. But just as obviously, to ask that question is to look in the right direction, for the Buddha is everywhere.

5. Kenneth Robinson, when he was Great Britain's Prime Minister of Health, told the Parliament that scientology was "potentially harmful" and a "potential menace."

6. There is no way to tell whether awareness continues after death, so we can conclude that it does not. But we are nothing more than awareness, since without awareness we experience nothing, not even blackness. Thus we do not survive death. Any moral system based on the certainty of reward and punishment in the hereafter is therefore fundamentally mistaken.

7. All citizens of voting age have the right to vote unless they are mentally disabled or have been convicted of a crime. Jim is a citizen of voting age and yet he said he did not have the right to vote. He's not mentally disabled, so either what he said is false or he's been convicted of a crime. But he also told me he's never been arrested, and it's impossible to be convicted of a crime and not to have been arrested. Thus, at least one of the things he said is false.

8. Just as without heat there cannot be cold, without darkness there can be no light, and without pain there cannot be pleasure, so too without death there would be no life. Thus it is clear that our individual deaths are absolutely necessary for the life of the universe as a whole. Death should therefore be a happy end toward which we go voluntarily, rather than an odious horror which we selfishly and futilely fend off with our last desperate ounce of energy.

9. As we have seen, proponents of national economic planning have been content to rest their case essentially upon dissatisfaction with existing economic and social arrangements and conditions, inferring that with a more rational, foresighted approach to economic life—national planning—we can do better. That inference, however, is a logical fallacy: One cannot derive the efficacy of Policy B from the deficiency of Policy A. If national economic planning is desirable public policy, it must be because it is both conceptually sound and consistent with the political reality in which it must necessarily function. Unfortunately, it is neither.

10. The classic trap for any revolutionary is always "What is your alternative?" But even if you could provide the interrogator with a blueprint, this does not mean he would use it. In most cases he is not sincere in wanting to know.

11. The eyewitness of criminal events plays an indispensable part in law enforcement. Without the intervention of third parties, there is little or no chance of rescuing victims, apprehending criminals, or solving crimes. Neither increases in police patrols nor harsher treatments by the courts can have much impact if ordinary people refuse to get involved, for it is the average person who has at his or her disposal the single most important resource for stopping crime—information. A critical priority in criminal justice policy must, therefore, be to increase the responsiveness of bystanders when they confront criminal behavior.

12. Once women actively begin to seek power, to seize the offensive, they will be formidable opponents. As newcomers to the establishment, they are not jaded by corrupt precedent nor lulled into dreary acceptance of the status quo. They are anxious to take on City Hall, to challenge the worse aspects of male authority—the corruption, the deceit, the arrogance—and to assert their own authority.

13. While General Grant was winning battles in the West, President Lincoln received numerous complaints about Grant's being a drunkard. When a delegation told him one day that Grant was hopelessly addicted to whiskey, the president is said to have replied, "I wish General Grant would send a barrel of his whiskey to each of my other Generals!"

14. An attorney is always free to consult law books. And a physician often looks up cases in medical texts. Everyone should be allowed the same sort of freedom of reference. So students should be permitted to use their textbooks during final exams.

15. Absolute music is perhaps the most eloquent and moving form of art, although it tells no "story." Abstract painting and sculpture are among the most magnificent products of human creativity, although neither of them has any "story," either. Therefore, the "story" it contains contributes nothing whatever to the excellence of a novel or drama as a work of art.

16. What prompted the Supreme Court of 1954 in desegregating schools to cast aside the accumulated wisdom of earlier courts and veer off into the tangled underbrush of sociology where even the best legal bloodhounds lose their trail in law? The explanation is obvious. It is that the court succumbed to the pressures that persuaded the Justices that a desegregation decision could perform a highly useful function in the realm of international relations and enhance the position of the United States in dealing with the nonwhite nations of the world.

17. JESS: The United States needs trade and military help. That's why the United States needs the friendship of other countries.

JANE: Sure. But the United States has forgotten something really important: that it must also help other countries. And that's precisely why we're losing some of our friends.

18. "[W]e must not regard what the many say of us, but what he, the one who has understanding of justice and injustice, will say, and what truth will require. And therefore you begin in error when you advise that we should regard the opinions of the many about justice and injustice, good and evil, honorable and dishonorable" (Socrates, in Plato's *Crito*).

19. "It is true also of journeys in the law that the place you reach depends upon the direction you are taking. And so, where one comes out in a case of law depends upon where one goes in" (Glanville Williams, in *The Sanctity of Life and the Criminal Law*).

20. "If I am mobilized in a war, this war is my war; it is my image and I deserve it. I deserve it because I could always get out of it by either suicide or by desertion" (Jean Paul Sartre, in *Being and Nothingness*).

21. PROFESSOR: What if I said that I am thinking of a primate that shares food and is monogamous? What would you say?

STUDENT: I'd say you were thinking of a human, a gibbon, or a marmoset.

PROFESSOR: Why?

STUDENT: Because among primates only humans, gibbons, and marmosets share food and are monogamous.

22. "[Chief Justice Warren Burger] is not the only justice on the Supreme Court who lacks a coherent, identifiable, judicial philosophy. . . . 'There are no strong philosophical bents on that court,' said University of Virginia Law Professor A.E. Dick Howard. 'Most of them are independent pragmatists who take each case as it comes' " ("Inside the High Court," *Time*, November 5, 1979, p. 64).

23. "Evolution is a scientific fairy-tale just as the flat-earth theory was in the 12th century. Evolution directly contradicts the Second Law of Thermodynamics, which states that unless an intelligent planner is directing a system, it will always go in the direction of disorder and deterioration. . . . Evolution requires a faith that is incomprehensible" (Dr. Edward Blick, in *21 Scientists Who Believe in Creation*).

24. "[O]ne of the distinct inconveniences or tragedies of human sexuality is that it endows us, and particularly the males among us, with a propensity to become exceptionally involved and infatuated with members of the opposite sex whom, had we no sexual urges, we would hardly notice. That is too bad; and it might well be a better world if it were otherwise. But it is not otherwise, and I think it is pernicious and silly for us to condemn ourselves because we are the way we are in this respect" (Albert Ellis, in *Sex without Guilt*).

25. "Young people can no longer get a bootlegged feeling of personal identity out of the sexual revolt, since there is nothing left to revolt against" (Rollo May, in *Antidotes for the New Puritanism*).

26. "[A]ccording to modern physics, radio is our only hope of picking up an intelligent signal from space. Sending an interstellar probe would take too long—roughly 50 years even for nearby Alpha Centauri—even if we had the technology and funds to accomplish it. But radio is too slow for much dialogue. The most we can hope from it is to establish the existence (or, more accurately, the former existence) of another civilization" (Patrick Moore, in "Speaking English in Space: Stars." *Omni*, November 1979, p. 26).

27. "If a being suffers, there can be no moral justification for refusing to take that suffering into consideration, and, indeed, to count it equally with the like suffering (if a rough comparison can be made) of another being. So the only question is: do animals other than man suffer? Most people agree, unhesitatingly, that animals like cats and dogs can and do suffer, and this seems also to be assumed by those laws that prohibit wanton cruelty to such animals" (Peter Singer, in *Animal Liberation*).

28. "Working at a paid job, any job, a woman is no longer just a family creature. . . . Hence, for women to work means relieving at least some part of their oppression" (Susan Sontag, *Partisan Review*, Vol. XL, 1973, p. 199).

29. "Experience indicates that purely voluntary efforts at self-regulation are not likely to be successful. There must be some enhancement mechanism by which violations of regulatory norms can be punished through collective action against the violator" (David Aaker and George S. Day, in *Corporate Responses to Consumer Pressures*).

30. "There is only one law which, by its nature, requires unanimous consent; I mean the social compact. For civil association is the most voluntary of all acts; every man being born free and master of himself, no person can under any pretext whatever subject him without his consent" (Jean-Jacques Rousseau, in *Social Contract*).

31. "We are asked to notice that the development of a human being from conception through birth into childhood is continuous; then it is said that to draw a line, to choose a point in this development, and say 'before this point the thing is not a person, after this point it is a person' is to make an arbitrary choice, a choice for which in the nature of things no good reason can be given. It is concluded that the fetus is, or anyway that we had better say it is, a person from the moment of conception. But this conclusion does not follow. Similar things might be said about the development of an acorn into an oak tree, and it does not follow that acorns are oak trees, or that we had better say they are. Arguments of this form are sometimes called 'slippery-slope arguments'—the phrase is almost self-explanatory—and it is dismaying that opponents of abortion rely on them so heavily and uncritically" (Judith Jarvis Thomson, in "A Defense of Abortion").

32. "It is the belief of this writer that ecology is a profoundly serious matter, yet most of the solutions suggested for environmental quality have, directly or indirectly, adverse effects on the poor and lower income groups. Hence, economic or distributive justice must become an active component in all ecology debates" (David R. Frew, in "Pollution: Can the People Be Innocent While Their Systems Are Guilty?").

33. Letter to the Editor arguing against the claim that Alabama's crime rate is abnormally high: "Alabama has never had anything within its borders, such as the assassinations of the Kennedy brothers, the King assassination, the horrible Manson murders, the Zebra and Zodiac killings of San Francisco, and the horrible Chowchilla kidnappings, the ghastly Watts riots, or the blackout lootings that occurred in New York City" (*Los Angles Times*, August 6, 1977).

34. "Language is the symbolic repository of the meaningful experience of ourselves and our fellow human beings down through history, and, as such, it reaches out to grasp us in the creating of a poem. We must not forget that the original Greek and Hebrew word meaning 'to know' meant also 'to have sexual relations.' . . . The etymology of the term demonstrates the prototypical act that is knowledge itself—as well as in poetry, art, and the other creative products—arises out of the dynamic encounter between subjective and objective poles" (Rollo May, in *The Courage to Create*).

35. Former Director of the Budget Burt Lance, defending his overdrafts at a bank in Calhoun, Georgia: "In a place like Calhoun, where you have a practice of overdrafts . . . 'overdraft' is not an ugly word."

II. Informal Fallacies

In this section, continue to look for conclusions and premises. But now also look for informal fallacies. More than one fallacy may be committed in each example, but try to focus attention on the one that is most glaring. When finished, go back and look for fallacies and analogies in the previous examples.

1. In January 2003, outgoing Governor George Ryan of Illinois commuted the sentences of 167 condemned inmates on the grounds that he felt a moral obligation to act because "the system is haunted by the demon of error." His critics immediately went on the attack and in one case noted the fact that the commutation took place one day before the opening statements were expected in the racketeering trial of Ryan's former chief of staff Scott Fawell. The critic noted: "What an amazing coincidence that he holds this nugget in his pocket until the last moment. . . . Why would he do that?" (Now the critic's comments do not comprise an argument, strictly. But they smack of at least two of the fallacies we studied in this chapter. Can you name them?)

2. Leader of women's rights caucus: "Look, we're all women here. We all share a desire to be free of the societal bonds that have traditionally shackled us. Of course, maybe some of you don't want your freedom. Maybe it frightens you. Maybe you would prefer to remain a social prisoner. But if you don't, if you want your freedom now, then endorse our proposal on demand!"

3. Superimposed over a picture of Supermodel Cheryl Tiegs, provocatively attired in a black velvet dress: "Isn't Black Velvet smooth? Just the thought of it can give you a good feeling. Black Velvet. Canadian whiskey. The smooth Canadian."

4. Editorial deploring state and federal failure to irrigate the Central Valley farmland in California: "Will huge areas of rich Central Valley farmland slip back into bleak, barren desert from which it sprang? Will acreage ranking in fertility with the valley of the Nile and the Fertile Crescent of the Tigris and Euphrates Rivers retrogress into sterile non productiveness? Will farmers go bankrupt, food production plummet, and a huge State and Federal tax base be wiped out? . . . These are not facetious questions. They stare starkly at California's future unless immediate, joint action is taken by State and Federal governments."

5. Bert Lance's reply to then Senator Charles Percy's observation that using a bank-owned plane to fly to football games and the Mardi Gras "hardly seems the atmosphere to conduct serious business": "Some people say the same thing about Washington, Senator!"

6. Former Congressional Representative Chet Holifield opposing a nuclear power limitations proposal: "You're going to hear arguments about safety. Those people (the ones proposing the limitations) are emotionally involved in this thing. It's difficult to bring logic to bear on emotionally disturbed people. Many of these people are fanatical. Their beliefs are based on misrepresentations."

7. In the 1960 presidential primaries, Democratic Senators John F. Kennedy and Hubert Humphrey engaged each other in West Virginia in what would prove to be a pivotal primary. At the time West Virginia had a large population of war veterans. To help the Kennedy effort, Franklin Delano Roosevelt, Jr., came into the state to speak on his behalf.

On one occasion, after noting Kennedy's splendid war record, Roosevelt said to the crowd, "There's another candidate in this primary. He's a good Democrat, but I don't know where he was in World War II."

8. "If we can justify the infliction of imprisonment and death by the state 'on the grounds of social interests to be protected,' then surely we can justify the postponement of death by the state. The objection that the individual is thereby treated not as an 'end in himself' but only as a 'means' to further the common good was, I think, aptly disposed of by Justice Oliver Wendell Holmes a long time ago. 'If a man lives in society, he is likely to find himself so treated' " (Yale Kamisar, arguing against a relaxation of the euthanasia laws in "Some Non-Religious Views Against Proposed 'Mercy Killing' Legislation").

9. When Roger Babson, whose prediction of the great stock market crash brought him renown, became ill with tuberculosis, he returned to his home in Massachusetts rather than follow his doctor's advice to remain in the West. During the freezing winter he left his windows open, wore a coat with a heating pad in back, and had his secretary wear mittens and hit the typewriter keys with rubber hammers. Babson got well and attributed his cure to fresh air. "Air from pine woods," according to Babson, "has chemical or electrical qualities (or both) of great medicinal value."

10. The alarmists have not succeeded in proving that radioactive fallout is dangerously harmful to human life. Therefore it is perfectly safe to continue our program of testing thermonuclear weapons.

11. I'm absolutely certain about how fast I was driving, officer, and it was well below the speed limit. I've had tickets before, and if you give me one now it will cost me well over a hundred dollars. And if I have to pay that large a fine I won't be able to afford to go ahead with a lifesaving medical procedure for my wife that is scheduled for next month.

12. You can't believe what Professor Threadbare says about the importance of higher salaries for teachers. As a teacher himself he would naturally be in favor of increasing teachers' pay.

13. A news release from the National Education Association (NEA) distributed in November begins with the following statement, "America's teachers see smaller classes as leading to a better job. . . .

"But the NEA, of course, is interested in having as many teachers in schools as possible.

"For example, in a 3,000 pupil school system with 30 pupils assigned to each class, the teaching staff would be approximately 100. But if the class size were reduced to 25 the total number of teachers would have to increase to 120. And in a time of shrinking enrollments, that is a way to keep teachers on the public payroll. . . .

"It is unfortunate that an organization with the professional reputation of the National Education Association should be so self-serving."

14. Congress shouldn't bother to consult the Joint Chiefs of Staff about military appropriations. As members of the armed forces they will naturally want as much money for military purposes as they think they can get. It is much like consulting a surgeon to ask whether or not she recommends an operation.

15. Was it through stupidity or through deliberate dishonesty that the administration has hopelessly botched its foreign policy? In either case, unless you are in favor of stupidity or dishonesty, you should vote against the incumbents.

16. Communists read *The Daily Worker*, which is known to be Fred's regular paper. And yet he stands there and argues for increased taxes to support the homeless. We know where he's coming from and therefore how spurious his argument must be!

17. Students who study at all will study each of their courses equally or study some more than others. This means that students who study at all will either get low grades in all their courses or fail some of them.

18. Keep up with the latest developments in alternative technology, environmental issues, holistic health, and human potential. . . . Listen in on conversations with humanistic innovators such as Margaret Mead, Frederick Leboyer, Daniel Elsberg, Allen Ginsberg, Elisabeth Kubler-Ross, and Bucky Fuller. . . . Look into *New Age*, the monthly magazine for people who want to make a difference in the world.

19. Seven months after Governor Broderick was elected the state had a budget deficit, the first in twenty years. Obviously, Governor Broderick is responsible and ought to be defeated in the next election.

20. We can't permit him to be arrested because he's one of us! When they arrest him they arrest each of us in a way. Fight for your rights! This police state action should be opposed in your own name!

21. I ask the jury to set free this man accused of murdering a policeman. If he is sent to jail, his poor children will have to grow up without a father, and will suffer the taunts of their schoolmates that their father is a convicted felon. Who could do such a thing to helpless young children?

22. When you join the Democratic Socialist Organizing Committee you're joining people like Michael Harrington, Representative Ronald Dellums, Gloria Steinem, Machinist's Union President Bill Winipesinger, Irving Howe, James Farmer, Joyce Miller, President of the Coalition of Labor Union Women, Harry Britt, San Francisco Commissioner, and Ruth Messinger, NYC Council Member. Most important, you're joining thousands of people you'll want to meet and work with in the struggle for a just society.

23. With the crime rate as it is, you must either carry a gun or live in constant fear.

24. Tom was seen in the vicinity of the broken window a few minutes after the accident, so he must be the one who broke it.

25. I am certain the war in Iraq was a terrible mistake. I heard the novelist Tom Clancey say so in an interview on PBS the other night.

III. More Informal Fallacies

Now, turn to your local newspaper or listen carefully to TV and the radio and see if you can find more examples of these fallacies. A good exercise is to make up some of your own. And a good place to find fallacies is in the opinion pages of your local paper—in editorials or letters to the editor.

A Suggested Procedure

1. Locate key terms and clarify them if necessary. We haven't discussed this, but it is an extremely important first step in analyzing any argument. It is not necessary (or possible) to clarify the meaning of every term in an argument, but it is necessary to be sure we know what the key terms mean so we're all operating "on the same page," so to speak.

2. Find the main conclusion: What's the point? This is usually, but as we saw not always, suggested by indicator terms. Ask the "Why?" question.

3. Look for argument support. What reasons are given to support the conclusion? Simplify these reasons somewhat (without oversimplifying them) and eliminate any irrelevant premises. You can tell they are irrelevant if they do not affect the conclusion one way or the other. That is, even if an irrelevant reason is true, it makes no difference to the argument.

4. Look for fallacies. We have considered several common fallacies in this section.

5. Evaluate the argument: Try to falsify. Examine the claims that comprise the reasons and ask whether they are plausible. Use your common sense. If someone were to say, for example, that "Magic Johnson is the best point guard ever to have played basketball," ask yourself whether or not such a claim could ever be proved true (or false). What would it take to substantiate such a claim? Try to think of counterexamples and exceptions to the statements that support arguments. Are the reasons consistent and coherent among themselves? Consider the relation between the reasons given and the conclusion said to follow from those reasons. Look for entailment or the lack of entailment. Ask yourself, "If this is true does that follow?" or "If I accept this claim, must I accept the conclusion (whether I want to or not!)?" Good questions are the basis of good criticism.

6. What's left? Where do we stand? This is the heart of the method of critical thinking that we have mentioned through-

> out. What remains after thorough criticism is more likely to be true than what we start with.

Remember to use this technique in criticizing your own arguments as well as those of others. The purpose of this technique is to find statements and connections among statements that can withstand criticism and that seem, therefore, to be true.

With this procedure in mind, we are ready to return to the problems involved in specifically ethical reasoning. You may recall that our chief concern in the domain of ethics is to avoid relativism and to assure ourselves that our ethical conclusions are justified by the reasons and evidence we provide for them.

NOTES

1. David Kelly, *The Art of Reasoning*, New York: W.W. Norton, Inc., 1988, pp. 96–97. Italics mine.
2. Harold Rugg and Ann Schumaker, *The Child Centered School*, Yonkers, N.Y.: World Book, Co., 1928.
3. J. L. Mackie, *Ethics: Inventing Right and Wrong*, reprint, New York: Viking Press, 1991.
4. Amy Binder, *Contentious Curriculum*, Princeton, N.J.: Princeton University Press, 2000.
5. Maureen Stout, *The Feel Good Curriculum*, Cambridge, Mass.: Perseus Publishing, 2000.

CHAPTER FOUR

The Justification of Ethical Claims

We turn now to the issue of justifying ethical claims, an issue that lies at the heart of ethical reasoning. When we are trying to resolve ethical conflict or determine which of several options is the right thing to do, we need to justify our decision by supporting it with cogent (strong) arguments, arguments that involve both facts and good ethical reasons.

Two pretenders are sometimes confused with justification because they appear to involve the same procedures as justification. But they are not at all alike, and we can have a much better idea of what justification involves if we begin by understanding its look-alikes, explanation and rationalization.

4.1 EXPLANATION CONTRASTED WITH JUSTIFICATION

Both justification and explanation seek to provide reasons why something is the case. We might try to justify having lied to our neighbor when she asked us whether or not we liked her ugly hat, for example. On the other hand, we might try to explain how the lie came about. In either case we give reasons, except that in the case of justification the reasons are supposed to support the claim that *one did the right thing* to lie. If one cannot justify having lied in this case that is because the reasons given are not good reasons. In the case of an explanation, on the other hand, we are trying to understand something we already know to be the case—the reasons we give increase our understanding; they do not support a conclusion that fails without that support. Explanations look just like arguments. The difference is that in an explanation we already know the conclusion; in an argument the conclusion is not known.

We can explain why so many Southerners in the antebellum South owned slaves and became indignant when told they must relinquish that ownership. We can understand, further, how these people in many cases persuaded themselves that they were right to own slaves, how they used bogus "scientific" information as "evidence" that because of a different cranial capacity blacks were inferior to whites and "therefore" deserving of their servitude. We can explain, and we can understand. But we cannot justify because we cannot find any good, ethical reasons to support the claim that slavery is right.

"Good Reasons" in Ethics

Good ethical reasons, generally, are relevant factual considerations (such as the fact that cranial capacity has nothing to do with intelligence) and normative claims that are difficult, if not impossible, to deny. A normative claim is a claim that presupposes a "norm" or standard, such as an ethical principle. Normative claims contrast with "descriptive" claims that, when true, we call "facts." I noted this distinction in the second chapter. Reasons are "good reasons" in ethics if they can withstand critical scrutiny and if they make the resolution of ethical conflict possible.

Of major concern to the objectivist in trying to make a case against the relativist are the ethical principles that must be incorporated into any attempt to justify ethical claims. Three such principles were covered in the second chapter, and we have seen that even though we find it difficult to reject them, at the same time, it is equally difficult to establish these principles and demonstrate that they are free from cultural bias. In the end, it would seem, the best defense that can be made for any ethical principle is the success of that principle in helping to resolve ethical conflict in a reasonable manner.

> The point I must insist upon is that rational principles are necessary for the possibility of the resolution of ethical conflict, and the validity of those principles is, ultimately, established by their success at resolving those conflicts ethically. It doesn't matter who put them forth or when or where. It doesn't matter how many people do, or do not, recognize or accept them. The

only issue worth consideration is whether or not the principles allow for the possibility of reasonable resolution to ethical conflict. If these principles allow us to resolve ethical conflict without acrimony and if they are worthy of acceptance by all disinterested, reasonable persons, then for all practical purposes they are sound.

The three principles I suggested in the second chapter are just such principles. At that time, you will recall, I defended the first principle, concerning respect for all persons, on the grounds that it is the cornerstone of any ethical system: Ethics would not be possible without such a principle; it would reduce to whimsey or a struggle for power. If, for example, we try to imagine a world in which there is no such ethical principle, we would find ourselves in a world much like Thomas Hobbes' "state of nature" in which life is "solitary, poor, nasty, brutish, and short." None of us would want to live in such a world if the alternative is a world in which persons are respected and treated fairly. To say, as I do now, that ethical principles are sound if they allow us to resolve ethical conflict reasonably is to say the same thing in other words. The test for these principles—all three of them—is to be found in the arena of ethical conflict and ethical decision-making. Despite the apparent circularity involved in such a test, it works well in the hard sciences in the form of what is called the "hypothetico-deductive method." It doesn't prove anything, strictly speaking, but, taken together with the consideration that we would all prefer a world in which ethical principles are upheld, it establishes those principles on fairly solid ground.

Thus, we must include sound ethical principles along with pertinent factual information in the class of statements that provide good reasons in ethics.

How Do We Recognize "Bad" Ethical Reasons?

It might help us to get a firmer grasp of what count as "good reasons" in ethics by considering what do *not* count as good reasons. The American philosopher Ronald Dworkin has addressed the issue and argues that there are four types of reasons in ethics that do not count as good reasons. He mentions rationalization and prejudice, which I have already discussed. To these two types he adds two more, "mere emotional reaction" and "parroting." Of the former he notes that

> We distinguish moral positions from emotional reactions, not because moral positions are supposed to be unemotional or dispassionate . . . but because the moral position is supposed to justify the emotional reaction, and not vice versa.[1]

The problem with human emotions, as C. G. Jung pointed out some time ago, is that "emotion is not an activity of the individual, but something that happens to him."[2] We cannot will to hate someone; it simply happens and then we do what we can to control it—which is always difficult. Even the "gentler" emotions, such as remorse, for example, do not seem to be a function of will. We hear stories of how the Nazis who guarded the Jews in the prison camps, and even the ones who gassed the victims, showed little if any signs of remorse after the fact. Just because something feels good, or is disturbing, doesn't take us very far in our attempt to resolve ethical conflict.

"Parroting," on the other hand, is simply repeating what we have heard others say—usually without giving it any thought. The temptation simply to repeat what "everyone knows" is strong, but as we have seen it is also fallacious. Just because "everyone else does it," or "everyone says that it's OK," we cannot consider this a good reason in ethical argument.

Good reasons, in contrast to these four groups of weak reasons, should appeal to what some have called the "universal audience," which is an imaginary audience of disinterested, intelligent people who would feel compelled *by the force of the argument* to accept the conclusion put forward.[3] These would be people like you and me who might find ourselves one day in a jury box attempting to weigh evidence to determine the guilt or the innocence of a defendant. I have incorporated this notion into my discussion of critical thinking earlier in the book, when I noted that the process of critically examining reasons that support ethical conclusions should yield ethical conclusions that would appeal to anybody.

4.2 RATIONALIZATION CONTRASTED WITH JUSTIFICATION

If one were to attempt to justify ownership of slaves in accordance with bogus "scientific evidence" we would not consider this justification at all; it is rationalization. Rationalization, like justification, involves the giving of reasons to support a claim that something is right or proper. In the case of justification, the reasons do support the conclusion because the reasons are true, or plausible, and the connection between the reasons and the conclusion is tight. Rationalization, on the other hand, is a weak form of argument in which a conclusion is held *despite the fact* that reasons do not support that conclusion. The attempted justification of slave ownership can be seen to be thinly disguised rationalization because it provides reasons for conclusions that are held independently of those reasons. We can debunk all of the "scientific" evidence that "supports" the claims that slaves are deserving of their servitude, but those who make those claims will probably maintain them anyway. The conclusion based on rationalization is held on grounds of emotion and prejudice, not reason. Psychologist Gordon Allport argues that when prejudice is involved, rationalization consists in "the accommodation of beliefs to attitudes."[4] We modify and adapt loosely held generalizations (beliefs) to accommodate our feelings (attitudes) about people and ideas, when it would be wise to reason to more accurate generalizations and modify our attitudes accordingly.

Several excellent examples of rationalization occur in Tolstoy's *War and Peace.* Early in the novel, one of the main characters, Peter, has just made a promise to Prince Andrew to stop mingling with the "wrong crowd" and living a dissolute life. Within moments of leaving Prince Andrew "a wild desire" came over Peter to join his friends in drinking and playing cards. He decides to "go to Anatole's rooms, persuading himself that his word is not binding, since he had promised Anatole one thing before he had promised Andrew another; that, take them for all in all, such pledges were merely conventional and had no meaning; that, after all, no one could be sure of tomorrow, or know whether some extraordinary accident might not sweep honor and dishonor, with life, into the grave."[5] In the end, he goes to Anatole's and makes a night of it!

Later in the novel, Tolstoy reflects on the nature of rationalization and our all-too-human desire to convince ourselves that whatever we have done was morally correct. In this case, Tolstoy has just described a scene in which the governor-general of Moscow has thrown a helpless political prisoner to an angry mob in order to create a diversion while he sneaks out the back door to escape the city prior to Napoleon's arrival. Tolstoy describes the governor-general's state of mind as he rides away:

> Comfortably rocked in his chariot, his body recovered by degrees, and as always the way, with the calming of the body, came calm to the mind. His mind suggested the most flattering arguments to soothe his spirit. They were not new ones; ever since the world was created and men began to kill each other, no man that has ever committed a crime of this character has failed to hush his remorse by reflecting that he was forced to it by his regard for the public good. Only those who do not allow their passions to get the upper hand refuse to admit that the good of the public can require such deeds. [The governor-general] did not for a moment blame himself for [the man's] death; on the contrary, he formed a hundred reasons for being satisfied with his own tact in punishing a malefactor, and at the same time pacifying the mob.[6]

Tolstoy is right, isn't he? We find dozens of ways to rationalize, to find "reasons" to support conclusions we are committed to for no reason whatever. The temptation is strong, indeed, and this is why we must be careful to distinguish between rationalization, which is all too common, and justification, which is the key to making a strong ethical argument, and why it helps as we attempt to justify our actions to reason things out with a neutral third party who can "see through" our attempts to support our actions with weak reasons.

We can see why rationalization is not like justification, even though the process sometimes appears to be the same.

> The rejection of the reasons given in the process of rationalizing does not affect the conclusion in any way!

In the preceding examples, Peter is simply determined to have a good time and the governor-general is determined to put his troubled mind to rest. In the more serious, real-life dispute over the issue of racial equality, we can show that cranial capacity has no relation to intelligence whatever and that, even if it did, lower intelligence does not imply "inferiority" or warrant servitude, and our opponent might maintain it anyway. If that were to happen, we would have a clear-cut case of rationalization, since it is obvious that the person does not hold to the conclusion *for the reasons given.* The claim is basically racist, and racism, as one form of prejudice, has no place in ethical reasoning. Justification, on the other hand, is a process that depends on reasoning. Ethical claims take the form of conclusions. Conclusions, as we know, are only as strong as the reasons that support them, and the argument itself only as strong as the connections between reasons and conclusions. If we reject the reasons as false or implausible, or if the connection between the reasons and the conclusion is not one of implication, we must reject the conclusion.

To see the differences between rationalization and justification more clearly, let us examine the reasoning involved in an example of attempted justification that clearly is a thinly veiled rationalization.

In the *Minneapolis Tribune* on October 18, 1990, there appeared a photograph of a bespectacled man leaving a court house in Bangor, Maine, with his daughter. The caption read as follows:

Hunter Acquitted of Manslaughter Charge.

Donald Rogerson and his daughter, Marcia, left Penobscot County Superior Court in Bangor, Maine, Wednesday after a jury found him not guilty of manslaughter in the November 1988 death of Karen Wood. Rogerson, 47, was hunting when he mistook Wood, 37, for a deer and shot her once in the chest behind her suburban home. The case pitted hunters against non hunters in an emotional debate. Wood had moved from Iowa four months earlier with her husband and twin one-year-old daughters.

One of the jurors was quoted after the trial as saying (in effect), "She should have known better: there were hunters all over that area." Let us assume that this is the juror's "reason" for voting "not guilty" in this case. Unfortunately, it is not a "good reason." Among other things, it is not logically relevant to the conclusion.

Consider:

(R) Wood shouldn't have been in her back yard with hunters all over the place.

(C) Therefore, Rogerson is not guilty of manslaughter.

There is no entailment whatever between this premise and the conclusion, as can be seen by the fact that the conclusion stated *or its contradictory* could be drawn with equal plausibility. The reason given might lead one to conclude that Karen Wood was careless, but it does not lead to the conclusion that Rogerson was not guilty of manslaughter. To say that he is not guilty of manslaughter is equivalent to saying that he didn't slay Karen Wood—which no one, including Rogerson himself, argues! There is simply no question that Rogerson was guilty of manslaughter. It was probably "involuntary" manslaughter, but it was manslaughter nonetheless. The jury's decision says, in effect, that Donald Rogerson did not kill Karen Wood, which is absurd!

A number of fascinating psychological and sociological reasons might *explain* why the jurors voted as they did. Karen Wood and her family were "outsiders" in the Bangor community. Hunting is pursued by a large number of Maine residents and, more importantly, it brings in revenue from out-of-state hunters to a state that depends on the tourist trade. There may be other reasons as well, all of which would combine to *explain* why the jurors voted as they did. That is, knowing these things will allow us to grasp why these people felt as they did and why they might vote in such an irrational manner. It is even possible that we might sympathize with the jurors to the extent that we can say we would have voted the same way they did in those circumstances. But none of these reasons comprise good, philosophical reasons that would *justify* the claim that Donald Rogerson was not guilty of manslaughter.

It might be said that the juror quoted "had his reasons" and that he was able to "justify it to himself." But this is a misuse of the term "justify." One does not justify one's actions "to oneself." One justifies courses of action to all reasonable persons (the "universal audience"), and the jury's decision—being irrational—was unreasonable. That is, no reasonable person would accept it. The best that can be said about the reason given for voting "not guilty" in the case of the death of Karen Wood is that it is an excellent example of rationalization. It is a reason given to support a conclusion held on nonrational grounds—as one suspects from the cryptic remark in the caption that "the case pitted hunters against non hunters in an emotional debate." The argument cannot withstand criticism, since, even if the reason given is true (which is doubtful) it has no bearing whatever on the conclusion. It is therefore not a good, ethical reason.

Attempts to Justify the Opposite Point of View

Can we provide "good reasons" to justify the counterclaim, namely, the claim that the jury was *wrong* to have found Donald Rogerson not guilty? That is, can we put together an argument that counters the rationalization of the juror we quoted earlier that is not, itself, just another piece of rationalization? What we need are reasons that are plausible and can withstand critical scrutiny. We tried this earlier, you may recall, in the case of outlawing radar detectors. Can we do so in the case of hunters who shoot unwary housewives in their backyards? Surely, we can.

Donald Rogerson was guilty of involuntary manslaughter because he was careless in the use of his rifle and shot Karen Wood. Even though the killing of Karen Wood was involuntary, in that it was accidental, Rogerson still bears responsibility because he should have taken precautions (such as getting close enough to determine that Karen Wood was not a deer). In killing Wood, Rogerson violated her right to life, which is incorporated in our first principle, and what he did was therefore wrong.

This argument is simple and straightforward. It appears to be free of bias and evidences no rationalization or special pleading. It incorporates facts (Karen Wood was shot by Donald Rogerson), reasonable inferences (Rogerson was careless), and an ethical principle (Wood's right to life) that is entailed by our first principle, which I have argued is the cornerstone of ethics. Thus, the conclusion that the jury was wrong appears to be justified in this case. Can it withstand criticism? Give it a try.

Recall some of the things I have maintained in the book thus far: It is imperative in ethics if we are to avoid "relativism"—the reduction of all ethical claims to personal opinion or cultural bias—that we eliminate such bias when we find it creeping into our attempts to justify ethical claims. Furthermore, the reasons we give must be capable of sustaining rational scrutiny and be compelling enough to warrant the consent of any disinterested bystander. "Good reasons" are not simply reasons that persuade *me;* they are reasons that should persuade *anyone*. They are, if you will, public reasons that must appeal to a disinterested third party, a "jury of our peers."

The cultural relativist, of course, will deny that this is possible. He will say that "good reasons" are simply reasons accepted by members of a particular culture but not necessarily by members of another culture. The relativist, then, might not criticize our argument as given here, but, rather, the attempt to justify *any* ethical claim. The relativist, you may recall, insists that the standards and principles of one culture cannot be "imposed" on another culture in the form of value judgments that arise within the former culture and are not recognized by the latter culture. Values and standards, it is said, are *relative to* particular cultures and cannot be employed to make "cross-cultural" value judgments. The same might be said about "good reasons." One might advance the following criticism: "We weren't there. We don't know what it was like. Who are we to say that the jury was wrong, anyway?" Is this a serious problem?

4.3 JUSTIFICATION IS NOT CULTURE-BOUND

The heart of our response to this criticism is contained in Nina's responses to Rick in our dialogue at the outset of this book. Basically, it comes down to the insistence that our justification, as a *rational* justification, is not necessarily culture-bound. That is, the reasons that we provide to support our claims are reasons that *anyone* should be able to accept or reject. If they are rejected, then others can replace them, but eventually through the method of critical rationalism, which I have adopted throughout this book, we can arrive at principles and standards that can function as good reasons in any ethical dispute. These reasons are deserving of acceptance by any rational person of good will who chooses to consider them dispassionately and with an open mind—that is, any member of the "universal audience." This is not a perfect system, but it can take us a long way toward reasonable solutions to ethical disputes.

The point I must insist upon is that ethical principles are necessary for the possibility of the resolution of ethical conflict and the viability of those principles is, ultimately, established by their success. It doesn't matter who put them forth or when or where. It doesn't matter how many people accept them or reject them. The only issue worth consideration is whether the principles are rationally defensible. If these principles allow us to support ethical claims and if they can withstand criticism and seem worthy of acceptance by other disinterested, rational persons, then for all practical purposes they are acceptable.

The juror in our example, of course, might not find our argument persuasive, but he *should* because good reasons are culturally neutral and should appeal to any reasonable person who takes the argument seriously and cannot find fault with the reasons given.

Once again, the focus of attention must always be on the reasoning process itself, and not the persons who put it forward or their cultural situation. The key question is not whether all, or only some, or any, people accept the reasons given. The key question is whether or not every person who hears the argument *should* accept it as sound—if only because there is no good reason not to do so.

Let me summarize the key points covered in this chapter.

---

1. Rationalization is the process of finding reasons (good or bad) to support a conclusion the writer or speaker is committed to on other grounds.

2. Explanation is the process that seeks to show why an incident or event occurred, but not necessarily that it was the right thing to do.

3. Justification is the process of combining factual evidence, strong argumentation, and ethical principles to establish that an action was the right thing to do.

4.4 CONFLICTING ETHICAL CLAIMS CANNOT BOTH BE JUSTIFIED

In closing, I should point out one rather important feature of justification: Conflicting claims cannot both be justified. If one claim conflicts with another, one or both of them must be false, and therefore incapable of being justified. The notion that a person "can justify it to herself" makes no sense. Justification is a public exercise and our reasoning must be submitted to a neutral audience and be able to withstand public scrutiny. Thus, for example, if the claim that "slavery is ethically wrong" can be justified, the conflicting claim that "slavery is ethically permissible" cannot be justified, whether or not a person "can justify it to himself." And *vice versa*. In some cases, neither claim can be justified—as would be the case if slavery were neither right nor wrong. And we recall that the claims themselves depend upon the reasons that support them: If the reasons are good reasons—that is, if they are plausible and/or can withstand critical scrutiny—the claim is justified; if the reasons are not good reasons, the claim is not justified. Thus, if an attempt is made to justify contradictory claims, the reasons for one, or both, of these claims must be weak.

A suggestion was recently made by the sociologist Michael Walzer that there are two kinds of morality, a "thick" morality and a "thin" morality.[7] Thick morality is permeated by cultural factors, history, and years of habits. A person in another culture is never in a position to judge whether or not thick morality is right or wrong because those outside the culture are not privy to the cultural factors involved. Thin morality, on the other hand, is what we might call a "core" of basic principles (like those I put forward in the second chapter) that are universally recognized and accepted or should be. Walzer is convinced that if we are sitting watching TV and see a news broadcast about people on the other side of the world being hauled off to prison without due process we would, naturally, be outraged—even if this were a common practice in that country. The reason for this outrage is that we recognize the violation of both the principles of justice and human rights in this case, and, whether or not the people involved in the action itself acknowledge them, we can say that this is quite simply wrong. This is an interesting view, and it allows for a compromise of sorts between the relativist and the objectivist. What do you think? Does it make any sense to you?

Food for Further Thought

The key to the position put forward in these pages against relativism is the notion that "good reasons" appeal to anybody at any time; they are not "culture bound." But is this possible? Is it possible to weigh reasons and assess them critically, as I have proposed in this book, *without* cultural considerations predominating? Isn't our cultural bias like a set of lenses through which we consider the reasons given to support ethical arguments: We are probably not even aware of them, but they color the way we hear and think about the reasons given. Because of this, what is "reasonable" in our culture is "unreasonable" in another. This is the point Rick makes in our second dialogue, and there is considerable truth in this criticism. Does Michael Walzer's suggestion help us out of this dilemma?

There can be no doubt that all of us, including the most dispassionate philosopher alive, is culture bound. But we must beware of the fallacy of bifurcation here! I am not saying in this book that it is possible for a person to free himself or herself entirely from cultural bias—we cannot accept the argument that we must either be *determined* by cultural bias or are *entirely free* of it. Cultural bias, together with the other subjective conditions I have mentioned throughout this book, does play a part in our ethical judgment. But the issue is not a matter of either/or; it is a matter of more or less. The critical question is whether we can free ourselves from those factors (by becoming aware of them, as I have proposed) *to a degree,* and if that is possible, it is sufficient for my purposes. This is what I meant when I suggested in the first chapter that objectivity in ethics (as is the case elsewhere) is a matter of degree. None of us is able to become completely free of subjective and cultural encumbrances, but some of us are better able than others, and all of us can improve.

Our goal, then, is to free ourselves as much as possible from cultural bias, emotional commitment, blind conviction, and narrow vision. We can do this by becoming aware of these factors as they influence our thinking, by becoming better informed on important issues, and by trying to think more critically in order to enable ourselves to consider ethical reasons fairly and with an open mind. This process must be ongoing and it is particularly difficult in ethics where we care so deeply about the issues involved. Because of this, it is extremely helpful if we submit our claims to criticism from others in a free and open exchange of ideas. Others frequently can help us see things we tend to overlook because we are too involved with the issues themselves.

Ask yourself whether this is a real possibility or merely a form of self-delusion. The key issue is whether you think the strength of arguments is merely a function of reasons that are irreducibly culture bound or whether there are reasons that do or should appeal across cultural boundaries. At this point you are in a better position to know where you stand than you were at the start of the book. You will be in an even better position to decide after you have attempted to work through some specific cases applying the procedures I have devised in this book.

EXERCISE

In weighing reasons and justifying ethical claims try to get at least one other point of view. I recommend that you make the strongest case you can for an ethical claim—any claim. Scrutinize that claim yourself, weighing reasons and strengthening the argument on your own. Now, submit the argument to one or two of your classmates and ask them to criticize your argument. (*Warning:* It is important not to *personalize* criticism. Remember that criticism of an argument is directed toward the argument itself and not the person putting forth the argument. Many of us find this process threatening until we have learned that we all benefit from it, so you might want to start with an ethical claim you do not feel strongly about!)

After the group discussion, return to the argument and strengthen it even further. You will be astonished at how much better your argument is after subjecting it to criticism than it was when you simply spun it out of your head. Don't forget to heed the warning, however!

NOTES

1. Ronald Dworkin, "Lord Devlin and the Enforcement of Morals," reprinted in Wasserstrom, *Morality and the Law*, Belmont, Calif.: Wadsworth Publishing, 1971, pp. 63–64.
2. C. J. Jung, *Aion*, Princeton: Princeton University Press, 1978, p. 8.
3. Ch. Perelman and L. Obrechts-Tyteca, *The New Rhetoric*, Notre Dame, Ind.: The University of Notre Dame Press, 1969, pp. 31–35.
4. Allport, *The Nature of Prejudice*, p. 14.
5. Leo Tolstoy, *War and Peace*, Geneva: Edito-service, Vol. I, Ch. X.
6. *Ibid.*, Vol. II, Ch. XLVI.
7. Michael Walzer, *Thick and Thin*, Notre Dame, Ind.: The University of Notre Dame Press, 1994.

CHAPTER FIVE

Ethical Argument in Action

5.1 THE ENVIRONMENT

Like Mom and apple pie, the environment is something everyone loves—right? Perhaps so, but not environmentalism or those environmentalists who have alienated some people in their active concern for protecting the environment. Indeed, the battles between environmentalists and anti-environmentalists have been rather heated at times, and like so many battles in ethics there is usually more heat than light. Perhaps I can remedy this situation by discussing at length a letter that appeared in a daily paper in Marshall, Minnesota, several days before Earth Day 1990, and then moving on to consideration of a typical case study involving some of the key issues in the controversy. I begin with the letter because it raises some interesting issues and because it will offer me an opportunity to show how to use the techniques developed in this book in a concrete example of ethical reasoning.

The letter reads as follows:

> I am properly concerned about pollution and other threats to the environment, nevertheless I maintain that the demands of the doomsday environmentalists would have us give up personal and national freedom to address highly-speculative [*sic*] theories. This would be both foolish and dangerous.
>
> There is no question that concerns about the environment have cost Americans tens of billions of dollars and led to a marked reduction in our nation's competitive position in world markets. Not satisfied with an array of taxes, regulations, and controls they have spawned, environmental lobbyists are gearing up for another assault on America's producers with their Earth Day 1990 scheduled for April

22nd. Yet, a growing number of scientific authorities now feel that many of the environmental claims are unsubstantiated hocum [*sic*].

For an example of environmental extremism, Earth Day 1990 Director Sen. Timothy Worth of Colorado has stated: "We've got to ride the global warming issue. . . . Even if the theory is wrong, we will be doing the right thing in terms of economic and environmental policy."

Professor Richard Lindzen of Massachusetts Institute of Technology and Jerome Namais of the Scripps Institute of Oceanography their [*sic*] claim that forecasts about global warming "are so inaccurate and fraught with uncertainty as to be totally useless to policymakers."

While environmentalists call for national and international controls to combat the frightening scenarios they repeatedly paint, I claim that many supposed threats, such as those involving ozone depletion, have never been based on credible evidence. University Professor Peter Beckmann has concluded that it is ludicrous to attempt to draw any firm conclusions from the skimpy data assembled to date.

The propaganda is so intense that President Bush has succumbed. When he proclaimed April 22 to be Earth Day 1990, the president suggested "the formation of an international alliance that responds to global environmental concerns." That indicates a willingness to transfer sovereignty that is more frightening than any environmentalist's wild claim.

Yours truly,
etc.

There are several vague key terms. What does the author mean, for example, by "personal and national freedom"? Are these economic freedoms, as suggested in the reference to the "reduction of the nation's loss of competitive position in world markets," or is the author referring to loss of "sovereignty"? Are these types of freedom related? If so, how?

There appear to be two conclusions connected, presumably, by the relationship (whatever it might be) between these two types of freedom. One conclusion is that we will lose our "personal and national freedom" if we listen to the "doomsday environmentalists"; the other, that President Bush's proclamation indicates a "frightening . . . transfer [of] sovereignty." Let us suppose the conclusions are somehow related. The argument would then be as follows:

(R1) Scientific evidence about pollution and "other threats to the environment" do not warrant measures leading to environmental protection.

(R2) Such protection, being unwarranted, would also lead to loss of personal freedoms, transfer of sovereignty, and a reduction of our nation's competitive position in world markets.

(C) Therefore [implied], we should not listen to doomsday environmentalists. *Or:* Action to protect the environment is not warranted at present based on the skimpy evidence.

What can be said about this argument as I have stated it here? In the first place, we must assure ourselves we have represented the argument fairly. Assuming that this is so, let us proceed.

To begin with, there is little evidence that this author has attempted to adopt the ethical perspective. The letter is filled with invective and loose language. Some of the adjectives (notably "spawned," "assault," "hocum," "doomsday," "foolish," "dangerous," and "frightening") comprise an appeal to emotion, since they slant the argument away from environmentalism without providing rational support for that slant. The author is clearly not neutral on this issue and seems to be little concerned about the long run. On a critical level, the argument assumes throughout that loss of "personal and national freedoms" is somehow related to a "marked reduction in our nation's competitive position in world markets." This needs to be argued, since (as I have noted earlier) there is some vague language here and the connection between these two items is not self-evident.

Another assumption, which we can readily grant since it accords with the first principle, is that we do not want to lose these "freedoms." A third and more important assumption (which we must question) is that this loss results directly from steps taken to protect the environment. This assumption smacks of bifurcation in that it presupposes that *either* we protect the environment, *or* we protect our personal freedoms and our position in world markets . . . *but not both.*

In the first reason stated, we note that the reference to "scientific evidence" smacks of illicit appeal to authority, since we are not told in the letter anything about the people appealed to—except that they are university professors—or whether we should lend their testimony any credence whatever. Further, these authorities have spoken only about ozone depletion, and that is not exhaustive of the class of actions we might collect in the phrase "pollution and other threats to the environment."

In addition, Senator Worth might insist that even if the increased costs cannot be avoided they must be incurred because, on balance, the consequences of failure to take steps to protect the environment may, in the long run, be even more costly—both financially and otherwise. Senator Worth seems to suggest in the quote given in the third paragraph of this letter that even if the danger to the environment is exaggerated, steps to protect it should be taken anyway, since it would be prudent to err on the side of caution in this case. The letter does not address this suggestion, so I shall take it no further; but it is a point worth noting, especially since it reflects one of the dimensions of the ethical perspective that the letter's author seems to ignore.

On balance, the argument is rather weak, and the conclusion is not warranted by the reasons given. The central connection that must be made to keep this argument afloat is that the money spent on steps taken to protect the environment invariably result in a "loss of our nation's competitive position in world markets," that is, that we cannot maintain that position and protect the environment at the same time. This bifurcation seriously weakens the argument, as it does any that would insist that environmental protection invariably results in loss of jobs, "quality of life," and world status. The tension between providing jobs and protecting the environment seems to lie at the center of many of the conflicts that have arisen in the controversy over the protection of the environment, and I shall return to this controversy in later case studies.

For the moment, let us take a fairly simple case involving some rather straightforward environmental issues to see how our principles and procedures are applied in assembling an argument rather than dismantling it.

Scott and Sharon want to buy a car, but they can't agree which one to buy. Scott wants a Mazda 6 because it's a "sporty" car with good pickup and speed, he has seen one in the showroom in candy-apple red, and he is smitten.

Sharon, on the other hand, wants a Honda Civic four door, and she has seen one at the dealer's in silver with a sporty little "bra" on the front end. The car of her choice is cheaper than Scott's, but they have agreed they can afford either car and they also agree that they could "live with" either car's appearance even though they have definite preferences. After considerable discussion, they agree to write down the reasons why they want the car of their choice and to take it from there.

Scott's reasons are as follows:

1. Safety
2. Environmental concerns, including economy (22/28 M.P.G.)
3. Performance (speed and handling)
4. Looks
5. Cost

Sharon's reasons are as follows:

1. Safety
2. Environmental concerns, including economy (34/38 M.P.G)
3. Performance (handling, adequate speed)
4. Looks
5. Cost

Since they have agreed that points #4 and #5 have been covered in prior discussions, they consider them a standoff. The argument works either way, they figure.

Eventually, they agree that point #3 is also a standoff because Scott has to admit that the Honda has adequate speed and handles well. However, he insists that the Mazda's added speed be considered a reinforcement of point #1 because it will allow the car to accelerate more quickly when passing and therefore avoid possible head-on collisions. Sharon counters that lower speeds are safer and whatever extra measure of safety is gained by the Mazda's additional power is lost because of the temptation to drive faster.

Next Scott introduces insurance company data that show that larger cars are safer in accidents; the driver and passengers suffer fewer serious injuries than they would in a subcompact of the Honda variety. Sharon counters with data of her own that show that subcompacts are involved in fewer accidents. In the end they concede this is another standoff because the argument seems to work both ways once again. Both sides can muster equally strong reasons.

Scott and Sharon both consider themselves environmentalists (not "doomsday environmentalists," just regular environmentalists).

Accordingly, they decide to purchase the Honda because it has much better M.P.G. figures. Their reasoning is as follows:

> Environmental concerns are one of the two most important factors in determining which car we will buy.
>
> Safety, the other factor, is a standoff.
>
> The increased fuel economy of the Honda is a decided environmental "plus." It will use less gas, which is a finite resource, and it will burn the fuel it uses more efficiently with less carbon dioxide emission, thereby doing less damage to the ozone layer–both key environmental considerations and concerns central to the ethical perspective.
>
> Therefore, we should buy the Honda.

Note how factual considerations enter into what is essentially an ethical argument. The argument is a strong one and the conclusion is entailed by the premises if we read the first reason as an ethical premise that states (roughly), "We should buy the car that is preferable from an environmental standpoint, all other things being equal."

The argument is strong, however, only because Sharon and Scott agree that they should protect the environment. They both accept the precept, "We should buy a car that is preferable from an environmental standpoint." What if either of them challenged that precept? Could it withstand criticism? Is it a *good* reason, one that *anyone* should accept? Remember, I have said repeatedly that an argument involving strict implication (as this one does) is only as strong as its weakest link. Let us see how strong this link is.

To test this precept, I shall use the method of "proposal and disposal" that I have suggested in the text. That is to say, I shall propose that the precept accepted by Sharon and Scott be accepted by everyone, and see if there are any good reasons to support this proposal. If we cannot find good reasons to reject, or dispose of, this precept, then we can suppose that it is worthy of acceptance by anyone and not just Scott and Sharon.

What reasons are there to protect the environment–which is the central claim in the precept we need to defend? As ethical principles, the three principles I advanced in Chapter Two would be excellent support for our precept here. The "environment" is the world in which all sentient creatures live–including, obviously, persons, whose rights must be respected in accordance with the First Principle. I have said that respect for persons is a necessary condition for ethics, and if this is so then it would appear that persons have a right to a clean environment. Polluted air damages our health and without clean water we would die, and life is the most basic of all human rights.

There may be such things as "animal rights" in addition, although I have not brought them into my argument. The notion of animal rights is troublesome, and I need not delve into the issue to make my point. I also need not consider the question of whether or not persons (and animals?) have rights to untrammeled wilderness or whether *future* persons (as yet unborn) have rights, although both of these claims are probable. It is enough for my present purposes to acknowledge the basic rights all persons have to a healthy life, which necessitates a clean environment, since this principle provides a good reason to protect the environment.

If this defense of my ethical principle stands, as it apparently does, then the precept I started out to defend earlier, to the effect that "we should protect the environment," can withstand critical scrutiny. Therefore, if Sharon can show that an economical car will burn less fuel and thus will protect the environment (more than a larger, less economical car would), her argument is quite strong, as we supposed.

5.2 COMPULSORY STERILIZATION

The following case is taken from Michael Bayles' *Professional Ethics*:[1]

> Ernest Friedman, a physician, has a patient, Georgia Hendricks, a young black woman with sickle cell anemia. She has recently delivered a baby girl. Her attacks have been fewer and less severe in recent years. However, Dr. Friedman has recently read an article indicating that if one discounts a few unusually low-risk women, women with sickle cell disease have an almost 10 percent chance of death during pregnancy. He has suggested sterilization to Georgia, but she has persistently refused. This new evidence about mortality makes him even more sure that she should be sterilized to avoid another pregnancy. He thinks that if he put the argument to her dramatically, she could probably be convinced to be sterilized. Should he ethically do so? Why or why not?

This is an interesting case. The key term, and one which requires clarification, is the term "dramatically." Just how dramatic does Dr.

Friedman plan to be? The key issue, however, is whether in putting an argument to his patient "dramatically" Dr. Friedman denies her status as a person—that is, her right to be respected as a person.

In a most important essay, to which I have referred earlier, Onora O'Neill argues that coercion, or manipulation, of one person by another constitutes a denial of the latter's status as a person; it denies that person's autonomy, or capacity to make moral judgments, which is what differentiates persons from things in the Kantian view and underlies the first principle I defended in Chapter Two.

The central issue, according to O'Neill, is whether or not there is genuine consent, which she defines as "consent to the deeper or more fundamental aspects of another's proposal." She goes on to argue, "To treat others as persons we must allow them *the possibility either to consent to or to dissent from what is proposed.* . . . The morally significant aspect of treating others as persons may lie in making their consent or dissent *possible.* . . . For example, if we coerce or deceive others, their dissent, and so their genuine consent, is in principle ruled out."[2]

The question in our present case is whether the physician denies the patient's rights as a person by presenting his argument "dramatically." Does he present his case fully and with vivid illustrations and examples in such a way that the patient could not possibly be expected to dissent? Or does he present the information fully but in such a way that *she* makes the decision whether or not to undergo the operation? The first case would be unethical; the second would be ethical—in the view presented here.

Fairness is not involved, since presumably the physician would treat *anyone* the way he treats this particular patient. Further, in allowing Georgia Hendricks to make up her own mind the physician can be said to adopt a rule that would work to the advantage of all, or most, who are affected by that rule.

Note here that if Dr. Friedman coerces Georgia Hendricks he not only denies her status as an autonomous moral agent, that is, a person, but he implicitly adopts a rule that would decrease the sum of human happiness, in Aristotle's sense of that term. Persons generally deserve respect as a *necessary* condition of ethical behavior. That is to say, such a rule, if adopted by Dr. Friedman, would allow that persons be coerced, or manipulated, whenever another person (presumably an "authority" or an "expert") determines that the situation warrants it. This very dangerous line of reasoning opens the door to all manner of abuses that would undermine ethical interaction among persons and decrease the sum of human happiness overall.

In this situation the principles imply that it is unethical under any circumstances to deny a person pertinent information that is necessary to make an informed choice. That is what "respect for persons" means, minimally, and it is one of the basic rights we have as persons. If Georgia Hendricks makes an informed choice, that is, if the "dramatic" presentation by Dr. Friedman is noncoercive, then we may assume that Ms. Hendricks would not upon reflection regret the decision. (That may well be the litmus test for coercion and noncoercion: Does one have regrets later on?) If Dr. Friedman coerces her into making a decision she will regret later, if she has not given her *genuine consent* to the surgery, then Dr. Friedman has done the wrong thing—regardless of the consequences. Clearly, it is imperative that we know how "dramatic" Dr. Friedman plans to be!

By way of summing up, let us use the techniques devised in previous pages of this book to put together a strong argument for the most reasonable conclusion we can reach in this case:

> Coercion involves the denial of one's right to be respected as a person and is therefore wrong. (Principle #1)
>
> Dr. Friedman's "dramatic" presentation to Ms. Hendricks does (does not) involve coercion.
>
> Therefore, Dr. Friedman should not (should) persuade Ms. Hendricks in a "dramatic" fashion to undergo sterilization.

Comment: As I have said, the key to this argument is the word "dramatic" and whether Dr. Friedman's manner of persuasion allows his patient to make her own decision whether or not to undergo the operation.

5.3 LAWYER'S PRIVILEGE

Consider the following case from Michael Bayle's book *Professional Ethics:*[3]

> Arthur Brown is a very busy and successful attorney. Ace Retailers has hired him to defend them in a suit by a customer. The complaint was filed twenty-seven days ago and Brown has not yet filed an answer, although he has had the case for over two weeks. When the president of Ace phones Brown, he tells him that he will not file an

answer until he receives a $20,000 retainer. State law requires that an answer be filed within thirty days or parties will be considered to have admitted all allegations of fact in the complaint. The president of Ace thinks the fee high even for a trial, and the case may be settled before going to trial. But since he doesn't have time to find another attorney, he sends Brown the check by courier. Is Brown's conduct unethical? If so, why? If not, why not?

This would appear to be a fairly straightforward case because it does not involve ethical conflict. If we were to weigh the reasons pro and con, the "pro" reasons for Brown's action would be exclusively a matter of short-run self-interest. It is difficult to see any good ethical reasons for what appears to be a case of extortion! The ethical perspective is nowhere in evidence. The "con" reasons take the form of violations of all three of the principles I defended in Chapter Two. This example will show how to apply these principles to a specific case.

Principle #1 (involving respect for persons) has been violated because Brown has been deceitful with the president of Ace Retailers and has violated the respect due the president, who is being coerced into paying what appears to be a rather steep fee for (what might prove to be) routine procedures.

Principle #2 (involving fairness) has been violated in that this form of extortion is grossly unfair to Brown's client, who is unable to exercise his free choice to replace Brown with another attorney. No one in the "original position" would approve of this sort of treatment of one person by another, and we suspect this would include Brown himself. That is, if Brown were himself the victim of this maltreatment he would certainly not approve. Thus, from the ethical perspective the action is suspect.

Principle #3 (involving the adoption of a rule that increases the happiness of those subject to that rule) has been violated because Brown cannot adopt an ethical rule to engage in this sort of practice, since it does not make anyone happy except Brown himself! Ironically, it may not make Brown happy. Let us see if we can make the case for this claim.

The action on Brown's part is not in Brown's best interest, though it might be in his short-run interest. In the long run, however, Brown is liable to manipulate himself out of business. The sort of treatment Brown accords the president of Ace Retailers will likely become known and Brown will gain a reputation as a crooked lawyer.

Potential clients will take their business elsewhere rather than fall victim to Brown's underhanded treatment. Whether or not Brown chooses to act ethically—and it is difficult to do so and survive as a "busy and successful attorney"—it would be prudent for him to act in accordance with his own long-run or "best" interest.

Let us put our findings in the form of a strong ethical argument:

> Consistent with respect for persons and fairness, one should adopt a rule that works to the advantage of those subject to that rule.
>
> Brown cannot adopt such a rule in this case, since his treatment of his client is both disrespectful—involving as it does extortion—and unfair.
>
> Therefore, Brown should not treat his client in the manner described.

An interesting question arises in connection with the application of the first principle to this case. Does the principle of respect for rights mean that persons are entitled to information they do not request? In this case, the president of Ace Retailers did not ask when Brown intended to file his brief—one suspects he did not consider the question necessary. That oversight cost him dearly, and we can say that the withholding of the information resulted in his being coerced into paying an exorbitant fee. But what if the withholding of information from someone works to that person's *advantage*? What about the use of placebos in medicine?

Suppose, for example, that a placebo could effectively cure a chronically ill patient and in the process save that patient a great deal of money. Clearly, the success of placebos necessitates secrecy—if the patients know they are taking sugar pills, the pills are not likely to work! Is it ethically right to withhold information in cases such as these when secrecy is essential to the success of the treatment?

This is a very complicated case, but I do not see how we could justify this sort of thing—even if it works—because it violates our first principle. That is, whether or not the placebo works (and there is a risk), the patient has been denied the right to make an informed choice and is therefore a victim of coercion.

Consider the difficulty of finding an acceptable rule to cover this case, a rule that will maximize the happiness of most persons affected by that rule. The placebo experiment might work in the majority of cases, although this is a moot point, but the rule would advocate the use of coercion as a means to a possible cure, making it an impossible rule to adopt, from an ethical perspective.

However, there is an added dimension in this case that is of central importance. A tacit understanding exists between a patient and a physician that may well provide a basis for ethical justification in the case of the use of placebos. The patient, it might be said, goes to the physician to be cured and presumably trusts the physician to do whatever is necessary to bring about that cure. If this "whatever is necessary" includes the use of deception, it could be argued that the patient *chooses* to be deceived. In this view, the patient waives his or her rights to complete honesty and total information if the remedy will work. This seems a bit bizarre, but we all do this every time we take a prescribed drug not knowing what chemicals the drug contains or what its effects might be; and even the most vociferous defender of free choice and autonomy might well agree that the doctor/patient relationship provides an exceptional case.

If we choose this line of reasoning, we could formulate and adopt a rule that patients may choose to suspend their right to informed choice in the interest of their own health, but it must remain the patient's choice and must not be forced upon him or her by the physician or else the patient's rights have been denied.

The argument would look like this:

> Coercion, as a rule, is ethically wrong.
>
> Coercion is involved when physicians deny their patients the right to make decisions involving their own health.
>
> Coercion is not involved, on the other hand, if patients waive their right to know every aspect of their treatment, if such knowledge would interfere with the success of the treatment.
>
> Medical treatment involving the use of placebos can only succeed if the patients are ignorant that they are receiving placebos.
>
> Thus, the use of placebos in such cases where patients waive their right to full disclosure is not coercive, and it does not violate any other ethical rules.
>
> Therefore, the use of placebos in such cases is ethically permissible.

5.4 WHISTLE BLOWING

Marlene and Steve live in Clotilda, California, a city of 80,000. Steve works at EMC, the local chemical plant, as a design engineer at a very good salary. They have a three-month-old baby who has just been diagnosed as having a rare liver cancer that may be untreatable. The young couple, devastated by the news, begin to question local agencies in an attempt to discover the possible causes of the baby's malady. They discover some startling facts: An unusually large number of cases of liver cancer has been reported in the past seven years in Clotilda, especially among very young children and infants, who do not usually contract this particular form of cancer. In addition, young women in the area have experienced three times the normal number of miscarriages in the past six years, and the area has had three and one-half times the usual number of birth defects in the past six or seven years.

Steve takes some water samples to the local pollution control agent, who has them tested. The results show that the water contains measurable quantities of dioxin, a known carcinogen, and Steve begins to suspect that the origin of this contamination is chemical waste that he knows EMC has been burying for the past ten or eleven years in a deserted landfill near the chemical plant. He suspects that leakage from the chemical waste is finding its way into the city's water supply. Subsequent investigation confirms this suspicion.

Steve approaches his supervisor at EMC to bring the problem to the attention of company officials in order to see what, if anything, can be done to clean up the dump site and eliminate the problem at its source. Upon pressing his inquiry to his increasingly uneasy supervisor, Steve realizes that the company has been aware of the problem for some time and has simply "covered it up." Steve's supervisor strongly urges him to "keep his mouth shut" and "do his job—or he won't have any job to do!"

Steve returns home and he discusses their options with Marlene. Above all else, they both want to do the right thing. This is the list of options they come up with:

1. Follow his supervisor's advice.
2. Quit the job and take another elsewhere.
3. "Blow the whistle" on the company to force it to clean up the

water and the landfill, even though this will result in Steve's losing his job—along with others who will probably be laid off when company profits dip as a result of the clean up.

4. Quit the job and take EMC to court to try to close the plant.

What should they do?

Steve and Marlene decide on the third option. Their reasoning is as follows: Alternative #1 would be prudent, but not ethical. On a personal level, additionally, they would find it difficult to go on as if nothing had happened knowing what they do. Alternative #2 would solve *their* problem but not *the* problem. Many of their friends in Clotilda would remain behind drinking contaminated water. Alternative #4 is impractical because Steve cannot afford the high costs of hiring a lawyer and the expenses of a protracted court battle against a wealthy chemical company.

Alternative #3 is the only acceptable alternative from the ethical perspective. Even though it will cost Steve his job, along with a number of his coworkers at EMC, Steve and Marlene reason that the company will be forced by local and federal officials, together with bad publicity, into cleaning up the landfill and stopping the leakage into the water supply. In addition, the residents of Clotilda will be made aware of a situation about which they are currently ignorant. They see the conflict as one between jobs, on the one hand, and the health of the city, on the other hand.

From the ethical perspective, Steve is concerned about the rights of others to a clean and healthful environment, and he adopts a rule that will maximize the happiness of the majority of persons affected by that rule.

At this point, Steve's argument would look something like this:

> The current situation involving the discharge of toxic chemicals is intolerable from an ethical perspective.
>
> The only effective option appears to be to blow the whistle.
>
> I have adequate documentation and I have good reason to believe that the situation will be remedied.
>
> Therefore, I should blow the whistle.

The situation is a bit simple as I have described it, of course. The reader is probably wondering about Steve's obligations to his family. As I presented the case, Steve and Marlene made the decision together, and I assume they would share a sense of obligation to the wider community and are prepared to face the harsh realities of finding a new job and paying what will probably be very large medical bills for their child. But I have ignored their obligations to their child. What about these obligations?

The new dimension doesn't change the ethical priorities in this case. Steve still has an obligation to blow the whistle, though he will surely lose his job as a result. The practical difficulties, although very real and pressing, are ethically irrelevant. As Steve and Marlene weigh the pros and cons of this situation, their love for their child and their awareness of the practical difficulties will surely enter in. But there do not appear to be any good, compelling reasons to agree with the objection that Steve and Marlene are ignoring their obligations to their child, or that this obligation overrides their obligation to the many who will contract cancer if they continue to drink contaminated water. From an ethical perspective (which, you will recall, is neutral) obligations are to *persons* and do not vary depending on who the person happens to be or what the relationship of that person is to the ethical agent. Steve and Marlene will surely *feel* a stronger obligation to their child than to 79,997 nonrelations in Clotilda. But this does not make the obligation more compelling from an ethical perspective, which requires neutrality.

But, surely it will be argued, I have ignored the rights of the baby. Perhaps the baby's rights must be considered equally with those of all other persons, but they must be considered somehow! I have simply ignored them to this point. Surely, the baby has the right to medical treatment, even if this treatment is likely not to help. I have stated in Chapter Two that human rights are a necessary condition to ethical action. Can't I be charged with inconsistency or even downright contradiction? (Steve and Marlene are doing the right thing to blow the whistle even though in doing so they ignore the rights of their child, which we have stated are a necessary condition to ethical action. This would appear to be a contradiction, indeed.) Let us reflect.

The only way I could agree that the baby's rights have been ignored is if Steve and Marlene deny the baby medical treatment, to which (admittedly) all persons have a right if that treatment has even a slight chance of saving the person's life. But even if I agree that medical treatment cannot be denied the baby without ignoring the baby's rights, it is not clear in this case that medical treatment *cannot* be supplied by Steve and Marlene unless Steve keeps *this particular job*. That is, the baby's rights are not being ignored *because* Steve blows the whistle and loses his job. (Beware the bifurcation: *Either* Steve keeps this job *or* he denies his baby's right to medical attention. This is simplistic.) The baby's rights would be ignored only if this series of events necessarily involved the denial of medical treatment for the baby, which they do not. There is no contradiction.

At this point, if Steve and Marlene were to put the argument together, it might look like this:

> The current situation involving the discharge of toxic chemicals is intolerable from an ethical perspective.
>
> Blowing the whistle appears to be the only effective remedy.
>
> I have obligations to the residents of Clotilda, but I also have obligations to my family.
>
> My obligations to my family require that I continue to make a living and try to find medical treatment for my child. Presumably, I can do both in another town.
>
> My obligations to the residents of Clotilda require that I blow the whistle, thereby informing them of the danger involved in drinking the city water, and, presumably, forcing the chemical company to remedy the situation.
>
> Therefore, I should blow the whistle.

I could, of course, persist in modifying the example by insisting that there is absolutely no way Steve and Marlene could provide medical treatment for their child unless Steve keeps his present job—which is highly unlikely. But if this were the case, then we would have to conclude that Steve and Marlene cannot do the right thing in this case because in doing one right thing (getting medical treatment for the baby or making it known that the city's water is contaminated) they must do a wrong thing (deny the baby's rights to medical treatment or deny the rights of the citizens of Clotilda to uncontaminated drinking water). This is an essentially *tragic* situation, that is, a situation in which there appears to be no right thing to do—although R. M. Hare would disagree, as we saw at the end of the first section in Chapter Two.

Fortunately, these situations are as rare as they are painful for those involved.

As if things weren't bad enough, the problem described here would be even more complicated, from an ethical perspective, if the chemicals did not pose a health hazard to the people of Clotilda, or if they only posed a *potential* health hazard. (Notice how these contingencies would weaken the various premises in Steve and Marlene's argument as I stated it earlier.) It would also be more complicated if the hazard were posed to nonhumans.

Take the case of "Butterflies vs. Industry," described by Ken Peterson (*San Jose Mercury*, October 25, 1979) as an example:

A large semiconductor company called Synertex proposed opening a $40 million research and manufacturing plant in Santa Cruz, California, across the street from Natural Bridges State Park. The plant would employ 350–400 workers. The problem arose when it was discovered that the plant would occasionally (about 20% of the time) release small amounts of hydrocarbons, sulfur, and nitrogen oxides into the air upwind from the park, where approximately 95,000 monarch butterflies congregate each year in their annual migrations. It was not known whether or not the fumes from the plant would harm the butterflies.

From an ethical perspective, should the plant be allowed to build at that site? Possibly a compromise might be worked out here (e.g., further testing of the effects of the fumes on the butterflies, relocation of the plant downwind, etc.). But if it is not possible to find a middle ground then the ethical conflict is in the form of a dilemma, one side of which concerns the jobs of 350–400 people and the other side of which concerns the damage to the butterflies and possibly to the ecosystem of which they are a part.

Some would argue that "animal rights" are at issue here, but I have not introduced this troublesome notion because it is not clear what this means, strictly speaking. Besides, it could be argued that humans have an obligation to protect the environment and its nonhuman inhabitants on the grounds that we should adopt rules that maximize human happiness—including, in this case, future generations.

Furthermore, even though we might agree that a person has a right to "make a living," or at any rate to the means necessary for survival, it is not clear that one could argue that a person has a right to a *particular* job. What do you think?

NOTES

1. From *Professional Ethics* by Michael D. Bayles, p. 89, © 1981 by Wadsworth, Inc. Reprinted by permission of the publisher.
2. Onora O'Neill, "Between Consenting Adults," *Philosophy and Public Affairs*, Vol. 14, no. 3. Italics in the original.
3. From *Professional Ethics* by Michael D. Bayles, p. 58, © 1981 by Wadsworth, Inc. Reprinted by permission of the publisher.

CHAPTER SIX

Cases for Discussion and Analysis

This chapter includes a number of case studies for purposes of analysis and discussion. The studies will be arranged in groups with some suggestions provided to help you with the first case in each group. You should not feel bound by the suggestions, but they might be helpful in getting you started.

Try to use the procedure outlined in the text when possible to help you prepare ethical arguments. Weigh reasons using the Socratic *maieutic* and try to focus your attention on the central question: What *should* a person (any person) do in this situation? Ignore the question of what a person might do (in fact). You might not agree that ethics should ignore practical considerations, but it will be helpful in working through the ethical issues if you put the practical questions on the shelf at first and ignore them. Ethical issues involving conflicts are extremely difficult to sort out and resolve. But if we are trying to decide what we *would* do at the same time we are trying to decide what we *should* do, the matter becomes even more complicated. Keep in focus the related questions: What *principles* are involved here? What is the *right* thing to do?

---

1. GENERAL ISSUES

G1. You are a member of a school board in a fairly large city in Ohio. One of the tenth-grade teachers who has taught at your school for six years and who has a reputation as a gifted teacher has just "come out of the closet" and announced that he is gay. The members of the school board want him fired. What should you do?

Suggestions: Focus on the key issue: What does respect for the teacher as a person involve in this case? Weigh respect for the teacher against the rights of the students and the possible harm that could come from confrontation with this teacher. Try to be realistic and consider carefully whether or not it is reasonable to expect harm to come to the students in this situation. Try to be clear what "harm" could mean in this context. Think, also, of the possible harm that could come to the teacher from being fired from this job.

G2. Jane has just been told by her doctor that she has contracted chlamydia from one or more of the young men she has had sexual contact with recently. Her concern is whether or not to tell her latest date, Dave, toward whom she has very strong feelings. She agrees, on her doctor's advice, to begin taking a prescription drug that should have an effect on the disease in a week or so, but she decides not to tell Dave for fear that she will lose him. In the meantime she decides to let things take their natural course. If they should sleep together, and she hopes they will, she's convinced herself "it's not like it's AIDS or something; if he gets it, he can get treated the same way I did." Did Jane do the right thing? If so, why? If not, why not?

G3. Sid Ramey is a member of a school board in a small town in Kansas. He has two children who are in the third and fourth grades and he is faced with a problem. A theater company from Kansas State University has been touring the rural areas staging plays for local schools for a very nominal fee. One of the plays they routinely perform is *Lysistrata,* a Greek play that is reputed to be rather bawdy (even in the "watered down" version the company has selected). The sentiment on the board is fairly strong to deny the group's request to perform at their school. They have heard from people in towns where the play has been performed that it is "pornographic" and "sexist." What should Sid do (1) as a parent, and (2) as a member of the school board?

G4. Nancy Quincey is on the city council of a small town in West Texas. The town has recently fallen on hard times and unemployment is rather high. Representatives from Texas Power and Light have approached the city council and proposed that they build and operate a nuclear reactor in the town. The plant will employ sixty-five people during construction and forty on a regular basis during operation. Nancy has heard that such plants can be dangerous and recalls the accident at Chernobyl. What should she do?

G5. On a hot August night in the Bronx, Paul Gilman and his friend Jesus Marcos were returning from a pool hall where they had spent the last four and a half hours playing pool and drinking beer. They decided to stop at a convenience store to pick up some more beer. Neither man remembered much that happened after that, but at Gilman's trial two months later it was determined that he had an argument with the sales girl over the price of the beer, pulled a gun, and shot her between the eyes. As he ran from the store, he shot two customers who were on their way in; one died instantly and the other was permanently injured. Eileen Thomas is sitting on the jury listening to the testimony and to the prosecutor, who insists upon the death penalty for Gilman. How should she vote?

G6. Sarah Douglas sits on the U.S. Commission on World Hunger. The commission is debating whether to increase U.S. aid to third-world countries to assist in relieving the problems of starvation in those countries. Amid the deluge of information about the numbers of starving people in undeveloped countries, Sarah is confronted by the following disagreement: One member of the commission argues that U.S. aid must be increased if America is to resume its place as a humanitarian leader in the world. He argues that it is a matter of self-interest on the part of the United States to "anticipate a problem rather than wait for it to become a crisis." Others argue that much of the money spent to alleviate world hunger is wasted because it never gets to the starving people; furthermore, even if it does reach those people, it simply exacerbates the real problem, which is population control. The argument insists that the money should be spent on birth control clinics and the education of ignorant populations rather than getting caught "on the treadmill of feeding the world's hungry masses." Money spent on feeding these people is "misguided humanitarianism," it is argued. Next to the possibility of a starvation crisis "the population explosion is considerably more threatening and terrifying to the rest

of the civilized world." How should Sarah vote on the issue of whether or not to increase U.S. aid to help reduce
world hunger?

G7. Jane Harney picks up some "pin money" by raising rabbits and selling them to local pet stores. Lately she has a
new client: A local laboratory has ordered a dozen, although Jane has heard that the lab will use the rabbits for
experiments in the development of perfumes. As new
chemicals are introduced, they are sprayed into the rabbits' eyes to determine their safety for human use. On occasion, the rabbits are blinded. Jane is not dependent upon
the income from the sales of the rabbits, but the laboratory has offered to buy twelve a week on a regular basis if
she can keep up with the demand. The money would go
a long way toward paying off some bills and letting her
put some away "for a rainy day." What should Jane do?

---

2. SPORTS

S1. At the age of seventeen William "Willie" Smith was caught
dealing drugs. While he was awaiting trial he enrolled at
a local junior college and later transferred to a small four-
year college in Iowa to study and to play football, which
he did very well. In the interim he was tried and found
guilty of the drug charge, but he was given a delayed sentence to allow him to complete his college degree. After
the completion of his degree he was to serve a nine-year
prison sentence. Willie's understanding was that his case
would be reviewed at the end of his college career and
that he would almost certainly be placed on probation if
he "kept his nose clean," which he did. He continued work
on his degree, and he played football so well he was
drafted by an NFL team in the ninth round. When it was
announced that he had been drafted, a reporter in his home
town ran a story about his brush with the law. In the en-
suing confusion the judge who had tried Willie's case three
years previously held a press conference and, noting that
athletes should not be given special treatment, repeated
her ruling that Willie was to serve nine years in prison as
soon as he completed his college degree. She insisted that
she never intended to review the case. The NFL team that
had drafted Willie announced soon thereafter that it was

no longer interested in Willie Smith. Did the judge do the right thing?

Suggestion: Remember that what is legal is not necessarily the same thing as what is ethically right. Courts and judges interpret the law; they are not necessarily concerned with what is right. Review our discussion in Chapter Two about justice as fairness. Is the judge's decision in this case "fair"? If we grant that punishment is necessary, is prison the only, or the best, form of punishment?

S2. Scott Boyer is a tennis coach at a small school near St. Cloud, Minnesota. He has a good boys' team; they have a chance this year to win their region and go to the state tournament. He knows that several other coaches in his region "stack" their lineups to place stronger players against weaker ones so that even though some matches are lost, the team totals will favor their teams. He has never done this, since the rules of his sport clearly state that teams are to play "in the rank order of ability," but he knows that if he follows this rule (while others do not) his team will almost certainly not win the regional tournament. What should he do?

S3. Pete Dimmer has been recruited to play football at Booster University. He is 6'3" tall, weighs two hundred pounds, and was an outstanding high school linebacker. At Booster, however, he is not as quick or as strong as his teammates and may not get to play the sport he loves. If he does not make the team he will lose his scholarship, and since he cannot afford to go to college otherwise, he will have to drop out. Most of Pete's teammates use steroids, and his coach has told him repeatedly that he must "bulk up," which he knows is an invitation to use steroids himself. (At the very least, none of the coaches has told him *not* to use steroids, and he can see for himself what an advantage they give to the other players.) What should Pete do?

S4. Patsy Wells coaches a women's basketball team in a small college in the Pacific Northwest. She has her eye on an outstanding college prospect, Julie, who is 6'2" tall and can run circles around every player in her conference. Julie will probably never make it to the state tournament because she plays for a weak team; as a result few coaches know about Julie's ability on the basketball court. The problem is that Julie has done poorly in her schoolwork in high school and will not be admitted to college unless she goes to a local community college for a couple of years and gets her grades up. If she does this, however, she will almost certainly play basketball, and other coaches will discover what a fine player she is. As a result, she will be heavily recruited and Patsy, whose budget is stretched to its limits, will almost certainly lose her to another school with a healthier budget. In addition, to win the conference, Patsy needs a power forward this year and doesn't want to wait two years. Julie really wants to play for Patsy and doesn't want to wait two years, either. As it happens, Patsy has a friend in the Admissions Department who is willing to alter Julie's records to make it appear that she has done acceptable work to this point. What should Patsy do?

S5. Monica Velez coaches gymnastics at the local high school in Peavey, New Mexico. She has a fairly good team, but she hasn't yet figured out how to get the best performance out of her gymnasts. She is convinced that she has three girls who are good enough to make the state tournament and possibly even get scholarship offers to college if only they would realize their full potential. Monica reads about the use of liquid B vitamins that can be administered just under the tongue and go to work almost immediately to provide extra strength and energy. A great many athletes, especially weight lifters, use the vitamins just before competition. Even though their use is still considered experimental, their success has been remarkable. The vitamins can be purchased at the local drug store, and Monica decides to give them a try.

At the next gymnastics meet, Monica gives her team the vitamins and they perform beyond her wildest expectations, winning the meet and qualifying two of her gymnasts for the state tournament. For some reason the girls are not the least bit curious about the drops Monica administers to them, so she decides not to say what they are. Monica has read that because the vitamins are administered to an extremely sensitive area, they have been known to cause cancer in some persons who use them. The label on the bottle of vitamins warns against "continued use" and "abuse" of the liquid, but Monica reasons that if her team uses the vitamins only before team competition, but not in practice, and if she has them stop at the end of the season, this will not constitute "continued use" or "abuse." In addition, her team will be able to perform better than ever and possibly even win the state tournament. What should Monica do?

S6. John Lenz coaches basketball at Willamette College. His teams have not done very well lately and his job is on the line. He is confident that this year will be a good one, however, because he has had an excellent year recruiting. He has watched several captains' practices involving three of this year's new players and one, Jeff Green, is outstanding. Jeff transferred to Willamette from a junior college where he was a Junior College All-American.

More than anything else, Jeff wants his college degree. He figures that he is not good enough to play professional basketball, and he looks forward to teaching and coaching young players. Jeff is John's advisee.

During fall preregistration for winter term, Jeff brings John a proposed course schedule that includes three difficult courses, one of which is a science course that involves a lab two afternoons a week during basketball practice. John recommends a lighter schedule, and one without science labs that conflict with practice. The problem is that the courses Jeff chose are required for his major, and they will not be offered again for another two years.

Jeff needs to take the courses he has proposed in order to graduate on time, and he is willing to take the science course even though he will miss practice twice a week. He suggests that he can practice on his own to make up for the missed practice sessions. John knows that missing two days of practice each week will reduce Jeff's effectiveness and make it very difficult for him to work well with the other players. Shooting baskets on his own in the gym twice a week is no substitute for practice with the team. It is even possible that Jeff will have difficulty with one or two of the courses and will not be eligible next year. John's dreams of an outstanding season seem to be going up in smoke. What should he do?

S7. An extremely gifted young professional basketball player by the name of Jason Mitchell has discovered that he has contracted the HIV virus and will be forced to retire from the game. In a very candid interview with a major sports magazine, he reveals that he has had sex with over two thousand women during his years on the pro tour, many of them after he may have contracted the virus. He is generally regarded in the press and by the public as a "hero" for coming forward and facing the issue honestly and without flinching. In addition, Mitchell had indicated that he would begin to speak out to young people about the dangers of AIDS and contribute a considerable amount of his own money to AIDS research.

In a later issue of the same sports magazine, one of the senior editors, Edith Wylder, argued that Mitchell should not be regarded as a hero for his involvement in what many people would consider irresponsible sexual behavior. Most people tended to ignore the fact that Mitchell may have infected any number of women with the HIV virus. Wylder argued that Mitchell's status as a hero or a villain will be determined by his actions in the future rather than his past behavior. She added that a woman would have been roundly criticized if it were revealed that she had slept with two thousand men! She argued that society was applying a double standard in this case, an argument substantiated by the revelation in the press that such behavior is quite common among professional athletes, one of whom boasted that he had slept with ten thousand women! What do *you* think?

---

3. MEDICINE

M1. Sally Curtis is a night nurse at the emergency room at the local hospital. Late one night when the emergency room is practically deserted, a policeman brings in a young man with a critical stab wound. The policeman has brought the man to this hospital because it is closest and, in his opinion, the young man could not have survived a trip to another hospital. The problem is that the young man has no identification, and there can be no way to know whether he has hospital insurance. From the look of him he has none. Sally has already been admonished several times for admitting patients without proper identification and proof of insurance. One more time and she is liable to lose her job. What should she do?

Suggestions: Try to keep the issue of short-run self-interest separate from the ethical problem here. Note, for example, how the issue changes if Sally is the sole support for her husband and three children or if she is single. Consider Sally's obligations to the hospital as well as her obligations to herself and to the young man. If Sally refuses the young man treatment and he later dies, is she an accessory to murder even though she didn't raise a hand against him? Can she *justify* her role in the young man's death by saying she did nothing to harm him, or is this *rationalization?* Put together an argument that could withstand criticism by a disinterested third person.

M2. Thomas and Emily have been married for forty-seven years. Emily has developed Alzheimer's disease, and her condition has deteriorated to the point where she doesn't recognize her husband when he visits her hospital room. While she is not in extreme pain, her husband finds it difficult to visit and see the way she is treated by the hospital staff and note the total lack of awareness she seems to have of her surroundings. It will not get any better, and Thomas recalls conversations he had with Emily in the early stages of her disease when they both agreed what they would do when "the time came." Recalling those conversations, and in the midst of a cloud of doubt and anguish, Thomas walks into Emily's hospital room, puts a .22 caliber pistol to her temple and pulls the trigger. Did he do the right thing?

M3. Dr. Herold Goldstein specializes in kidney diseases. He has three patients in critical condition, all of whom are on dialysis machines waiting for a kidney donor. One of the patients is a seven-year-old boy. Another is a thirty-five-year-old mother of three children whose husband has recently filed for divorce. The third is a former all-pro cornerback who now, at the age of forty-two, coaches football at the local high school. A donor is found who can provide a kidney for one of the patients, but the likelihood is that another will not be found in time to help the other two patients. Which of the three patients should Dr. Goldstein select for the donor kidney, and why?

M4. Elaine Fedder, a sixteen-year-old pregnant woman who wants an abortion, visits the local Planned Parenthood organization. She requests that they not notify her parents that she has been there. Later that day, nurse Clyde Davis phones Elaine at home. When Elaine's mother answers, he does not leave his name or that of the Planned Parenthood organization, but he does leave his phone number, asking Elaine's mother to have Elaine phone him when she returns. Elaine's mother immediately phones the number and discovers that it is the Planned Parenthood organization. She confronts Elaine and forces her to have the baby and marry the baby's father, a seventeen-year-old high school student. Was nurse Davis unethical in leaving his phone number? Why or why not? Do parents have an ethical right to be informed of medical treatment for their children? If so, at what age does that right cease, or doesn't it?

M5. Asher Bausch and his wife are both Ashkenazi Jews. They went to the local genetics unit to be tested for the chances of having a child with Tay-Sachs disease. This recessive genetic disorder is untreatable and produces blindness, motor paralysis, and other symptoms leading to death, usually before the age of three. The tests showed that Asher was a carrier, but that his wife was not. While he and his wife were not at risk of having a child with the birth defect, Asher's brothers had a 50 percent chance of being carriers, and if either of them married an Ashkenazi Jew, the chances were 1 in 30 that the wife would be a carrier and so the odds were 1 in 60 that they would have an affected infant. Dr. Cloe Dunlop asked Asher to send his brothers a letter that the genetics unit had prepared suggesting that they be tested for the carrier status. Asher became upset and refused. He felt ashamed and could not bring himself to tell his brothers. Would it be ethical for Dr. Dunlop to write the brothers and recommend to them that they have genetic screening? Why or why not?

M6. A psychiatrist, Janell Jensen, is treating Irwin Johnson, who was referred to her as being near a nervous breakdown. After a few sessions, Irwin confesses to having murdered a child six months before. Janell does not think Irwin will murder again and thinks that she can assist him, whether or not he turns himself in to the police as he is thinking of doing. What should Janell do? Why?

4. LAW

L1. Scott Koll is representing his client who has been convicted on a criminal charge. They are now before the judge for sentencing. The judge asks the clerk if Koll's client has a previous criminal record, and the clerk says he has not. However, Scott knows that his client does have a record. While he is trying to decide what to do the judge says, "As this is your first offense, I shall give you a suspended sentence." What should Scott do? Why?

Suggestions: Think about whether telling an untruth when asked a direct question is a lie in the same sense that silence in a case such as this might be. Are both unethical? Equally so? Keep Scott's self-interest out of the issue until the end. If Scott's silence is tantamount to a lie, would it be wrong in this case? Can Scott simply say to himself: "The clerk made the mistake; it's not my problem"? Would this be rationalizing? Make a case for Scott, one way or the other, that can withstand your own critical scrutiny and that of your classmates.

L2. Leslie Jacobsen is a young and talented lawyer who has been with the Public Defender's Office in Los Angles for seven years. She has recently been assigned to defend Amos Pritchard, a man accused of a series of brutal murders. This is the first time she has been assigned to such an important case with sole responsibility for the client's defense. In her conversations with Pritchard, however, it becomes clear to Leslie that the man is guilty not only of the murders mentioned in the indictment, but also of several others, and that he is likely to kill again if found not guilty and released. She tries to convince Pritchard to plead "not guilty by virtue of insanity" and seek psychiatric help. He refuses and becomes outraged at her suggestion that he might be "nuts." Just before Pritchard's case is scheduled to come to trial, the police arrest a homeless drug addict who confesses to the murders Pritchard has been accused of. Leslie knows she can get her client off, but should she? What should she do?

L3. Paul Schlehr is an activist lawyer with political ambitions. A couple of years ago he prosecuted a case that struck down the racial and sexual discriminatory practices of a local corporation. He is also vice-president of a local environmental organization. The corporation's factory is now being forced to close due to new local regulations on pollution. The local black organization, which considers him its lawyer, wishes to join the corporation's management in attacking the local regulations on pollution so that the factory can remain open. Paul would represent the blacks who obtained jobs as a result of his earlier case. The suit will probably be opposed by the environmental organization to which Paul belongs. What should he do? Why?

L4. Attorney Jake Sanders is representing Humboldt, Inc. in a contract negotiation with the Joiner's Union. They are fairly close to an agreement on a wage increase, but both sides are intransigent. To get things moving, the union's chief negotiator, Marcia Lockhardt, phones Jake and offers the following compromise: Humboldt will agree to release ten employees who do not belong to the union and who are not essential to the company's operations. In turn, Marcia promises that the union will accept a wage agreement closer to Humboldt's terms, and Humboldt could save more than enough to meet the union's wage demands. The contract could be settled without further delay. What should Jake recommend? Why?

L5. Amy Pivec, a young and upcoming corporate lawyer, has been subpoenaed to appear before a grand jury seeking an indictment against Trilux Corporation for violations of antitrust laws and six counts of extortion and bribery in connection with an earlier case. Amy is close friends with Michael Brown, an executive in Trilux with whom Amy has spent considerable time. Michael is one of the executives named in the indictment, and Amy will be asked to reveal information Michael told her in strict confidence not as his lawyer, but as his friend. If Amy does not reveal the information she will almost certainly be found in contempt of court and may face disbarment proceedings. She knows that some of the information Michael has disclosed to her will get both Michael and Trilux into serious trouble. What should she do?

---

5. BUSINESS

B1. You are an engineering consultant to mining firms. Surestrike Mining hires you to do two jobs for $5,000 each. One is to evaluate a potential mine you are already familiar with; you are sure that your report will be negative. Should you accept the job?

The second job is to evaluate a productive mine. You discover that the mine has moved to an adjacent property owned by East Texas Mining Company and that Surestrike does not have the mineral rights to the coal being mined there. You report to Surestrike that they are infringing on the mineral rights of East Texas Mining. They thank you and pay you the money they owe for your fee.

Six months later you discover that Surestrike is still mining under the property owned by East Texas Mining and that they have not notified the latter company of your findings. Your contract with Surestrike provided that you would not disclose any findings to a third party. What should you do?

Suggestions: Try to keep the legal and the ethical issues separate, and keep both separate from the practical issues! Whether or not a contract you signed is legally binding, it may or may not be ethically binding. Ethics is a matter of principles and when laws conflict with ethical principles some would argue that ethics must take precedence. Martin Luther King, Jr., argued this in his "Letter from a Birmingham Jail." In any event, the issues must be kept separate. Would it make any difference in this case if you were single or a married person with several other people dependent upon your income? Along this line, suppose that you know you will be blackballed in the mining industry if word gets out that you have "snitched" on Surestrike. Is this an ethical consideration, or a purely practical consideration?

B2. Kevin Black is an aspiring young management trainee with a large chemical company in New Jersey. His supervisor calls him one day and tells him that he is to assume responsibility for the burial of waste materials that are known to contain toxic substances that cause cancer in humans. He is told to take care of the waste material in the cheapest and quickest way possible. Research leaves him with only three options: (1) Bury the waste near a small town of 350 people. There is a probability of 40% that the waste material will leak into the drinking water of the town and prove dangerous to the health of the residents. This way is the most expensive. (2) Bury the waste in a rural area that is destined to become a golf course and is currently mostly farms. There are several dozen families in the area of the waste site. The waste will almost certainly seep into the groundwater because of the high sand content in the soil. This way is almost as cheap as the third option. (3) Bury the waste in a swamp near a city of 7,500 where the likelihood is 2 in 10 that the waste will leak into the water supply and harm the residents. This is the cheapest way to dispose of the waste chemicals. What should Kevin do?

B3. Jill Gunderson is employed as a research technician by Goodhealth Drug Company. She ran a series of tests of Colstop on mice. She wrote in her report that many of the mice developed cataracts and lost hair when injected with the drug. She later saw the report that went to top level management of Goodhealth and also to the FDA. Several of her sentences had been deleted and the cataracts were not mentioned. She reported the omission to her superiors, who became angry and told her to go back and change her original report so there is no mention of the cataracts. Jill earns a good salary at the job and is the widowed mother of three children. Jobs of this caliber are hard to find. What should she do? Why?

B4. Your company sells only in the state of New Wyoming. State law does not prohibit marketing your cola in "giant quarts," which is an advertising phrase that describes a quart bottle. However, a survey conducted by your firm indicates that 40% of cola buyers think that the "giant quart" is larger than the standard quart. Should you market your "giant quart"?

B5. Steven Boyd, a second-year MBA student in a top business school in the Chicago area, believes he probably will go to work right after graduation for one of seven firms that already have offered him a job. He continues, however, to arrange interviews through the school's placement office. He reasons that the experience is valuable and that he may even turn up a better job.

Two companies invite him to New York City to visit their home offices. Steven plans the visits on consecutive days. He stays a night in a hotel in New York, for which one of the firms had agreed to pay, since it scheduled his interview at an early-morning hour. But Steven charges both firms for the full cost of his round trip transportation. He tells himself that because each firm said he should send in an expense account, he is not getting anything the companies did not expect to pay. One firm did not even ask him to submit receipts. Steven interprets this to mean that the firm really intended to give him the money as a gift. Did Steven act unethically? If so, why? If not, why not? If you were an employer, knowing what you do about Steven Boyd, would you hire him? Explain fully.

B6. Margaret Larsen is the personnel director for a large manufacturing firm that has recently built a plant in the heart of Chicago's South Side. The company is hiring both skilled and unskilled employees and Margaret decides, on her own, that the company should hire a large proportion of blacks since the plant is located in a predominantly black neighborhood. The proportion of blacks who apply for jobs is about 67%, but Margaret manages to hire 83%, although the percentage is slightly less in the skilled group than in the unskilled group. Her hope is that some of the unskilled workers will be promoted and the percentages will even out eventually. Should Margaret have taken it upon herself to adopt such an aggressive hiring policy? Is it a policy that her company should adopt whether or not Margaret had decided to do so? Explain fully.

---

6. THE ENVIRONMENT

E1. Pete Stigma is a foreman for the International Logging company in Sweet Home, Oregon. His company laid off seventy-four people in the last two years and closed one of its three mills. Recent legislation setting aside millions of acres of first-growth pine to save the spotted owl will result in more layoffs and perhaps the closing of another mill. Pete's job is relatively secure because he has been with the company for many years, has seniority, and will retire soon anyway. But the jobs of many of his friends are in jeopardy.

Pete's company orders him to begin logging away from the gravel roads in areas that he knows are within the habitat conservation area (HCA). Because of the remoteness of the area, however, and the rapidity with which new machinery makes it possible to clear-cut the area, he knows that the operation probably won't be spotted until it is completed. At that time, if the operation is noted, the company will pay a small fine and simply pass the cost of the fine along to the customers with a slight price increase. Pete has always considered himself a conservationist and loves the wild area in which he has grown up. But the "preservationists" back East have made him increasingly angry because of what he considers their persistent meddling in an area that they have never even visited. They are the ones responsible for the legislation that would bind the hands of the logging industry and result in so many lost jobs. If he obeys his company's orders he will be doing what any loyal employee should do, and he can save some jobs in the process. What should he do?

Suggestions: Much of the ethical tension in environmental issues centers around the issue of jobs versus the environment: Is it possible to conserve the environment while we save and/or create jobs? Focus on this issue, and watch for red herrings as was discussed in the text. Also, ask yourself whether or not a job is a "right" every person has *as a person.* The Greeks, for example, thought that work was demeaning, but since the so-called Protestant work ethic began to prevail in this country in the nineteenth century, work has seemed necessary for self-esteem, if not for sustenance. However, if a federal fund, say, could provide enough money to sustain people comfortably without the need to work, would the world be a worse place to live in than it is now when everyone expects to hold a job? This is a key issue in this debate.

E2. Blane Jackson is the CEO of MacDougal Baggot, one of British Columbia's largest forest-products firms. His company has been clear-cutting the forest that comprises 80% of the land in that area for many years, and has recently expanded its cutting operation into an area near the village of Kyuquot on Northern Vancouver Island. The 249-mile-long island is being logged faster than any other part of British Columbia. Of its eighty-nine largest watersheds, only six remain uncut. Blane's company plans to begin operations in one of those areas next month, but there have been a number of protests by environmentalists and members of the Kyuquot tribe who reside in the area. Some of these people have met with Blane in his office and requested that he spare this area, a pristine wilderness on which the native people depend for their livelihood, chiefly hunting and fishing. A committee appointed by the provincial government to study old-growth forests across the province has recommended that logging in those areas be

suspended for two years. Blane is not bound by that rec-
ommendation, nor by the demands and requests of the
people who have met with him. Furthermore, two years of
delays will cost his company thousands of dollars, since
the equipment is nearby and roads have already been cut
to the logging areas. Such costs will almost certainly result
in layoffs and increased costs to his customers, which will
hurt his competitive edge. What should Blane do?

E3. Judge Leslie Bright is hearing an appeal in the Reserve Mining case involving a Minnesota taconite mining company
that has been permitted for years to dump 67,000 tons of
taconite tailings daily into Lake Superior. The Minnesota Pollution Control Agency, the Environmental Protection Agency
of the federal government, and the U.S. Justice Department
have insisted that the company cease its operations because
the tailings comprise a health hazard to the residents of the
area, who depend on the lake for their water supply. Also,
they contend, the plant in Silver Bay, Minnesota, discharges
particles into the air that can cause asbestosis, mesothe-
lioma, and various forms of cancer. Reserve contends that
the evidence that the plant's activities pose a health threat
is not compelling and cites evidence from Dr. Arnold Brown
that "with respect to both air and water, the levels of fibers
in the discharge is not readily susceptible of measurement"
and cannot be shown, therefore, to be dangerous. Because
a danger cannot be shown to exist, their lawyers contend,
the plant should not be closed. Such a move would cause
considerable economic distress in the area, since Reserve
Mining employs 80% of Silver Bay's 3,000 inhabitants. What
should Judge Bright do?

E4. On March 28, 1979, Fred Dwyer, a maintenance engineer
at Three Mile Island nuclear power station near Harrisburg,
Pennsylvania, was shaken by an alarming series of events.
At 4:00 A.M. a minor device in the reactor cooling system
malfunctioned causing a series of valves to close, the main
pumps to stop, and the power generating turbine to shut
down. Fred checked his gauges and noted that the heat in
the reactor was rising rapidly. Apparently an auxiliary
pump was supposed to start automatically, but someone
had inadvertently left the valve shut and water could not
enter the reactor to cool it down. In a matter of moments,
a safety valve opened because of increasing temperatures

in the reactor, but the valve failed to shut down. As a result, steam was discharged into a drainage tank, and the reactor became so hot it shut down automatically. Only eight seconds had passed, but Fred was shaking and his heart was pounding in his chest. Lights and alarms were going off everywhere. Fred and his fellow engineers were convinced that the water pressure within the reactor was continuing to build so they shut down the pumps. The temperature in the reactor rose even higher.

As events became clearer later on, Fred realized that four operator errors had occurred along with two mechanical failures. Although they had come within an hour of a core meltdown that would have resulted in the death of thousands of area residents for whom evacuation plans were hopelessly inadequate, disaster was avoided by a series of steps Fred and his fellow engineers had taken subsequent to the events described. Nevertheless, his confidence in the safety of nuclear plants was completely shaken.

As a result of this experience, Fred moved his wife and two small children to central Iowa and took a job with an electronics firm for $4,500 less in salary. He subsequently published several articles pointing out the dangers of nuclear power and the desirability of alternative sources of energy. Did he do the right thing? [*Hint:* The ethically right thing is not the same thing as what was right for *Fred,* which is to say, what made Fred feel good. Recall that the ethical perspective requires neutrality. The key issue here is this: What should anyone in Fred's place do?]

E5. Ralph Griffin is the CEO of a paper mill in northern Minnesota. He has been reading a great deal lately about acid rain and the depletion of the ozone layer, and since his company has operated for years without scrubbers on its smokestacks he knows that he is contributing to the problem. Scrubbers are very expensive and while their cost could be passed along to his customers, it would take years to pay for the new equipment and in the meantime his company would lose its competitive edge in the paper industry. This is especially true since none of the other companies in the area use scrubbers: They are not required by law, thanks to delays in clean-air legislation in Washington. Ralph has a deep love for the area where he has lived his entire life, and he wants to make sure his grandchildren can enjoy the region for years to come. What should he do?

E6. In 1978 it was discovered that chemicals buried since the early 1940s in an abandoned section of the Niagara Falls area called Love Canal were seeping into the drinking water in an area of town where a new school and a fairly large residential complex had been completed a few years earlier. Several adults showed signs of incipient liver damage, young women in certain areas close to the canal experienced three times the normal rate of miscarriages, and the area had three and a half times the normal incidence of birth defects. Hooker Chemical and Plastics Corporation admitted to burying the chemicals, but insisted that the burial was in strict accordance with regulations on the books at that time. In addition, they had warned the city of Niagara Falls not to build a school on that site, since the construction could damage the integrity of the clay bed in which the chemicals were buried. They had even received a signed statement from the city exempting the company from any responsibility in the event that injury or death to persons or damage to property arose from the construction of a school and a residential complex in that area. Some argue that Hooker Chemical should bear the cost of cleaning up the area, estimated to run around $250 million. Still others argue that we should all pay the cost because we all use chemical products daily, many of which are produced by Hooker Chemical at its Niagara plant or elsewhere. A federal "Superfund" exists for the purpose of cleaning up toxic waste such as that buried in Love Canal. Hooker Chemical argues that the city of Niagara Falls should pay the cost since they knew the danger going in and went ahead and built a school on that site anyway. What do *you* think?

7. STUDENT DILEMMAS

SD1. Sally lives off campus with three other women. One evening she receives a phone call from a man who identifies himself as "David," and who tells her that he got her name and number from one of Sally's roommates. David wants to ask Sally out for dinner and a movie. The trouble is, David did not get Sally's number from her roommate; he got it from the campus directory. He has never seen Sally but has heard that she is a great date. Is there something wrong here?

Suggestions: This seems to be a fairly straight-forward issue, but think about what David has done. You may say that people do that sort of thing "all the time." But ask yourself whether this constitutes a good ethical reason for justifying David's actions. Examine closely the precise nature of David's action and focus on what is consistent with ethical principles. In the end, you might do exactly what David did, but would it be *right?*

SD2. Mary is in a small advanced music theory class taught by a blind instructor. During her first test she is aware that her classmates are passing notes back and forth and comparing answers to test questions—unbeknown to the instructor, who has told the students that he trusts them and that they are on their honor to take the test honestly. Should Mary tell the instructor what is going on?

SD3. Fred works for campus security to help pay his way through college. He has a key to every room on campus and is able, and willing, to check professors' rooms prior to major exams to see if there are any tests lying around on the professors' desks. When he finds them, he copies them and sells them to his fellow students. He reasons that if the profs are "dumb enough" to leave their tests lying around, then there's nothing wrong with his picking up some extra money to help with his college costs. Is he right?

SD4. Charlie is an English major and is in his final semester before graduation. He must pass a fairly rigorous math final to get the credits he needs to graduate. He has always had difficulty with math and is barely passing this course. A week before the final, he is talking with another student in the Union who tells him that he can get Charlie the questions for the final. It seems the professor is known to give the same three finals in rotation every year and it is a sure thing that this year's final will be the same as the one two years ago. Should Charlie take his friend up on his offer?

SD5. Sharon is not a writer; she's an art major and hates writing with a passion. But she has a ten-page paper due for her freshman English class on an assigned topic and she knows she can go "on line" and buy the paper. Should she do this?

GLOSSARY

Argument As this term is used in this text, it refers to a series of statements that are connected by a logical relation called entailment. One of the statements is called the conclusion of the argument and the other statements (one or more) are called reasons or premises. The term contrasts with exposition, which is a series of disconnected statements that do not support a conclusion (see Chapter Three).

Claim Claims are either relative to the speaker or the speaker's culture, or they are nonrelative. A nonrelative claim professes to be about our shared world and may be true or false: It is open to verification or falsification by persons other than the speaker himself or herself. Some nonrelative claims are stronger than others in that the evidence in support of them is more likely to be true. The argument in this book seeks to support the view that ethics can involve nonrelative claims that are as strong or as weak as their rational support.

Justification A process of rational argumentation by which claims are supported. This term usually refers to ethical judgments that purport to be true, that is, to ethical claims. The term contrasts with rationalization, which is an attempt to find good reasons to support positions that one holds for bad reasons—that is, personal or emotional commitments one is reluctant to abandon. (For both of these terms, as well as a discussion of good reasons, see Chapter Four.)

Objectivism (also nonrelativism) This term contrasts with subjectivism or relativism (see later) and refers to the neutrality of claims, that is, their lack of dependence upon the speaker or writer. Objectivism, that is, the doctrine, has reference to the thesis that claims are *objective,* that is, capable of independent verification. I follow Karl Popper (who follows Immanuel Kant) in insisting that knowledge claims (including ethical claims) are "objective [when they are] *justifiable,* independently of anybody's whim: a justification [in turn] is 'objective' if in principle it can be tested and understood by anybody . . . the *objectivity* of scientific statements [for example] lies in the fact that they can be *intersubjectively tested*" (Karl Popper, *The Logic of Scientific*

179

Discovery, New York: Harper and Row, p. 44). To the extent to which a claim is objective it is not subjective and *visa versa*.

Rationalization   See Justification. Rationalization is the process of finding reasons *after the fact* for conclusions we hold for personal reasons (that is, reasons that have no universal appeal) and are reluctant to abandon.

Relativism (see subjectivism)   Refers to the relationship of beliefs to the one stating the beliefs. Beliefs are said to be relative to the speaker (in the case of subjectivism) or to the speaker's culture (in the case of cultural relativism). From a systematic point of view, both forms of relativism pose the same difficulties for one who seeks to defend objectivism, or the view that ethical judgments, for example, are not mere beliefs and are not simply relative to persons or cultures.

Subjectivism (see relativism)   One form of relativism in which claims merely reflect the personally held beliefs or opinions of the speaker.

INDEX

Act utilitarianism, 52, 54–55
Ad hominem fallacy, 109–110
Ad populum fallacy, 98–99
Agendas, 104
Analogies, 112–113
Anthropology, 33–34
Appeal to authority, 102–104
Appeal to emotion fallacy, 104–105, 143
Appeal to ignorance, 82
Appeal to the people fallacy, 98–99
Aquinas, Saint Thomas, 46
Areté, 40–41
Argument chains, 91–92
Argument webs, 92–93
Arguments
   defined, *xv*
   development example, 23–25
   elements of, 83–84
   evaluating, 89–90
   evaluation examples, 95–98
   examination exercises, 113–120
   explanation as, 127–128
   versus feelings, 78–79
   rationalization as, 131
   structure, 84–86
Aristotle, 40–43
Assumptions, 25, 88–89
Authority, 103
Autonomy, 48–49

Begging the question fallacy, 101–102
Bentham, Jeremy, 52
Bias
   in history, 21–22
   overcoming, 38

purging of, 31–32
   versus reason, 3
   recognizing, 14
Bible, 19
Bifurcation fallacy, 107–109, 143
Blanchard, Brand, *xviii*
Burden of proof, 81–83
Business ethics exercises, 170–173
Butterflies versus industry, 157

Capital punishment, 46, 47, 60
Car buying, 144–147
Care. *See* Ethics of care
Causation, 110–112
Character, 40–41, 42
Circular reasoning, 101–102
Claims
   acceptance criteria, 79–80
   conflicting, 137–138
   context, 10
   evaluating strength, 14–15
   truth of, *xv–xvi*
   types, 11–12
Coercion, 48–49, 148–149
Common sense, 25
Community, 40–41, 43
Compulsory sterilization, 147–149
Conclusions
   connecting with premises, 90–91
   and justification, 133
   terms for, 84–85
   uncovering, 88–89
Condemnation, 37–38
Consent, 148
Consequences, 52, 62–64
Contradiction, 107

181